Outdoors

Once upon a time, there was a sharp line between where a home-owner's living quarters ended and the outdoors began. The first area was a figurative castle, to be decorated with the best furnishings money and imagination could provide; and the second was, by default, an ill-defined space where a window box of geraniums, a backyard picnic table, a barbecue, a sandbox and a swing set vied for attention. But no longer. As house design in general has become more flexible, and as living styles have grown more informal, outdoor spaces increasingly have been assigned to specific uses, and furnishing them now calls for due care.

The practical benefits of this kind of expansion are obvious. When you turn the space just outside your door into an attractive environment for dining, entertaining, reading, or musing on the day's events, you extend the physical limits of your house. As the photographs in the following prologue suggest, the ways of annexing space can be very modest — witness the rustic man-made pond on page 5; or they can be of a scale that requires the help of skilled professionals, as in the sleek pool and patio overleaf.

The basic approach to designing outdoor spaces can vary considerably, too. Indoors and outdoors can be joined as an integrated whole, as was the aim in creating the *trompe l'oeil* gazebo and garden on page 6. Or the outdoors can be appropriated in a way that firmly sets it apart from the style and mood of the rest of the house: The contemplative, Asia-inspired garden adjoining a high-rise Manhattan apartment *(page 9)* is one example; the airy pavilion overlooking the Côte d'Azur *(page 6)* is another.

Different as these patios, porches, terraces and yards are, all of them share one feature and broadcast it as a message: Like conventional rooms indoors, spaces outdoors benefit from being enclosed — set within walls, or fences, or screens, or plantings to ensure a sense of privacy and removal from the world beyond.

A quarter-circular swimming pool set into a tiled courtyard between house and un-
tamed woodlands becomes the visual
center of this New York country retreat. The
site's southern exposure provides direct
sunlight for both the outdoor area and the
large-windowed interiors that flank it. By
night, underwater lighting in the pool turns
the space into a shimmering grotto. Lush
greenery, weathered cedar cladding and a
triangular-shaped screen-wall that draws
the long sloping roof line to earth skillfully tie
the house to its natural surroundings.

A man-made reflecting pool transforms a city lot into a thriving habitat for extravagantly colored bog plants and golden orfes, a species of carp. The pool was excavated to a depth of 2½ feet and lined with sturdy rubber sheeting to hold the banks and retain the water. Blue flagstones, laid around the borders, give a finished look to edges and provide a secure walkway.

This asymmetric water garden in the backyard of a Virginia residence looks like an example of nature's finest handiwork, but it is in fact the product of human effort with pick and shovel. Roughly 180 square feet in area and 3 feet at its deepest, the pond has been lined with flexible polyvinyl chloride (PVC) sheeting. Rocks brought up in the digging now anchor and conceal the edges of the liner. And a recirculating pump and some plastic tubing send a trickle of water over the lilliputian waterfall near the back center, to keep the flow aerated and make a pleasing noise.

Looking like a Victorian gazebo, this structure is the mirror image of an equally imaginative but solid summer beach house that rises in the foreground. Together they enclose a very private, tranquil outdoor living room. Wedge-shaped raised flower beds spill over with plantings to give the area a luxuriant look, and the shifting patterns of light and shadow through the latticework make the space ever-interesting.

A white pavilion, erected on a frame of curved metal tubing, screens the balcony of a 19th Century seaside villa above the Mediterranean. The outdoor room, which is an extension of the master bedroom, can be as public or as private as its owners choose: The sheer white muslin curtains slide open and closed. The balcony floor doubles as the roof of an open-air dining room on the main floor below.

Double-decker screened porches add substantially to the outdoor living spaces of this 19th Century Delaware house, which is tucked into a 50-by-100-foot beach-front lot. To integrate the new with the old, the owner has incorporated traditional gingerbread drollery into the architectural design. Among the artistic touches are pine-tree cutaways in the porch balustrades, stars in arched frames of the screens, and a trim board of wooden lambrequins across the upper story.

The tiny terrace of a small apartment in
Florence, Italy, is carved out of unused
space in and over the eaves. Because every inch counts here — visually and physical-
ly — minimal furnishings have been designed, using almost-transparent metal mesh
and frames. The table is nothing more
than a shelf projecting out into the air.

A setback adjoining a New York City
high-rise apartment becomes a restful retreat. The terrace was first lined with
heavy plastic sheeting to protect the roof below; then a white pebble path, tree tubs,
and planting beds of lightweight soilless
soil — such as perlite or vermiculite —
were laid out. Plantings, designed to be
attractive year-round, include evergreen pachysandra and blue-toned junipers,
and several trees whose forms are lovely
even when leafless. A white stone sculpture
of a Buddhist deity, bolted to the terrace
wall, overlooks the scene.

Built around a Santa Fe patio, this massive adobe wall becomes a single, integrated means to providing a raised fireplace, comfortable seating and privacy.

Other Publications:
THE ENCHANTED WORLD
THE KODAK LIBRARY OF CREATIVE PHOTOGRAPHY
GREAT MEALS IN MINUTES
THE CIVIL WAR
PLANET EARTH
COLLECTOR'S LIBRARY OF THE CIVIL WAR
THE EPIC OF FLIGHT
THE GOOD COOK
THE SEAFARERS
WORLD WAR II
HOME REPAIR AND IMPROVEMENT
THE OLD WEST

*For information on and a full
description of any of the Time-Life Books
series listed above, please write:*
Reader Information
Time-Life Books
541 North Fairbanks Court
Chicago, Illinois 60611

This volume is one of a series that features home decorating projects.

Outdoors

by the Editors of Time-Life Books

TIME-LIFE BOOKS □ ALEXANDRIA, VIRGINIA

YOUR HOME

SERIES DIRECTOR: Gerry Schremp
Deputy Director: Adrian Allen
Deputy Director for Text: Jim Hicks
Series Administrator: Barbara Levitt
Editorial Staff for *Outdoors*
Picture Editor: Jane Jordan
Designers: Susan K. White (principal),
Edward Frank
Text Editors: Dale M. Brown, John Newton,
Peter Pocock
Staff Writers: Adrienne George, Kathleen M.
Kiely, Denise Li, Glenn Martin McNatt,
Jane A. Martin
Copy Coordinator: Robert M. S. Somerville
Art Assistant: Jennifer B. Gilman
Picture Coordinator: Renée DeSandies
Editorial Assistant: Carolyn Wall Halbach

Special Contributors: Lynn R. Addison,
Sarah Brash, Anne R. Grant, Feroline Burrage
Higginson, Wendy Buehr Murphy

Editorial Operations
Design: Ellen Robling (assistant director)
Copy Room: Diane Ullius
Production: Celia Beattie
Quality Control: James J. Cox (director),
Sally Collins
Library: Louise D. Forstall

Correspondents: Elisabeth Kraemer-Singh
(Bonn); Margot Hapgood, Dorothy Bacon
(London); Miriam Hsia (New York); Maria
Vincenza Aloisi, Josephine du Brusle (Paris);
Ann Natanson (Rome).

THE CONSULTANTS

Frederick L. Wall, a furniture maker and sculptor,
is an instructor in furniture design at the Corcoran
School of Art in Washington, D.C. His work has
been featured in many exhibits and publications.
Mr. Wall has been responsible for designing and
building many of the projects in this volume.

Jane Krumbhaar, a landscape designer, learned
her craft in England at the side of professional gardeners there. She now operates a landscape contracting and design firm in the
Washington, D.C., area.

First printing. Printed in U.S.A.

Published simultaneously in Canada.
School and library distribution by Silver Burdett
Company, Morristown, New Jersey 07960.

TIME-LIFE is a trademark of
Time Incorporated U.S.A.

Library of Congress Cataloguing in
Publication Data
Main entry under title:
Outdoors.

(Your home)
Includes index.
1. Garden structures. 2. Outdoor furniture.
3. Exterior lighting. I. Time-Life Books.
II. Series: Your home (Alexandria, Va.)
TH4961.094 1985   643'.55   84-28106
ISBN 0-8094-5520-X
ISBN 0-8094-5521-8 (lib. bdg.)

CONTENTS

Designs for outdoor living

Like the rooms within a house, the living space outside can be shaped and furnished to suit a multitude of purposes. Some areas will need to be strictly utilitarian: for parking cars, for concealing trash cans, for storing garden tools. Yet even a small lot can also provide pleasant places for dining, gardening, or simply luxuriating in the fresh air and beauty of the outdoors.

The secret of creating outdoor living space that is useful, fun to be in and wonderful to look at is to produce a carefully considered, detailed design before turning a spadeful of earth. The genesis of the design is twofold: You must decide what you want from your yard, and you must determine what it offers you to work with.

List all of the purposes you may want your yard to serve, from providing herbs for the kitchen to furnishing play space for children. The list will depend on your family's ages, hobbies and habits. Make your list exhaustive, even if your yard is too small to accommodate everything you want; later, you can set priorities and pare down the list.

To get a clear idea of what you have to work with, you must catalogue and measure the principal physical features of your property—the house, walks, trees, fences and so on. Record this information in a scale drawing called a site plan, like the top sketch at right (using graph paper makes drawing such a plan easy). In finding the dimensions of your lot, do not assume that existing fences or hedges are on the property lines; they may in fact be several feet removed. If you are uncertain of your boundaries, try to obtain a plat, a scale drawing of your property prepared by a professional surveyor. One may be on file with your local government. If not, you may wish to hire a surveyor to mark the boundaries; misplacing a structure or even a group of plants can be a costly mistake.

The site plan should show where sunlight falls at different times of day during the part of the year when you will be making most use of the outdoors. Note also the prevailing winds that you might want protection from. Look for unsightly views you would like to block — and pleasant ones to highlight or expand. And of course you will need to know the locations of utility lines *(top right)*. While working up your site plan and wish list, find out what legal constraints you may face. Local regulations often affect the height and placement of fences or the design of ornamental pools. Your neighborhood may have its own set of restrictive covenants that are part of your deed.

With a complete site plan and the list of needs and wants, you can create a use plan — like the lower drawing at right — that matches different functions to specific locations. Work from inside your home out as you analyze the possibilities, taking into account the factors noted on the site plan. Unappealing views from windows can be obscured by fences or shrubs. A terrace usually is near a door to the house. Gardens need sunlight, play areas should be visible from inside the house, and storage areas can be tucked away out of sight. Consider getting rid of badly positioned features. It may be worth cutting down a tree or ripping up a concrete walk if you free space for better use.

The use plan provides the basis for the final design. However, more than one good design can evolve from the same use plan, as the illustrations on subsequent pages show. Your design decisions, besides being influenced by the characteristics of the site, will be expressions of personal taste. Consider how the possible man-made elements — terraces, walks, lighting, benches — will harmonize with various trees or other plants. Think of plants themselves as materials comparable to wood, brick, flagstone or gravel, and evaluate them for the same factors: cost, availability, texture, color or maintenance requirements. If, for instance, you want privacy and you also want to keep maintenance to a minimum, a wood fence may be more satisfactory than a hedge that requires frequent pruning.

After your design is on paper, you can get a more complete sense of its total effect by taking wood stakes and string into your yard to mark the outlines of walks, shrub groupings and other large features. Try to imagine how the yard will look at all seasons of the year, and after five or 10 years of growth, when plants will have increased greatly in size. If you do not have the time or money to execute your entire design immediately, establish priorities and carry out the projects over months or years. If you make changes in the design as you go along, give them as much thought as you did the original plan, so that your outdoor space will become as useful and beautiful as you can make it.

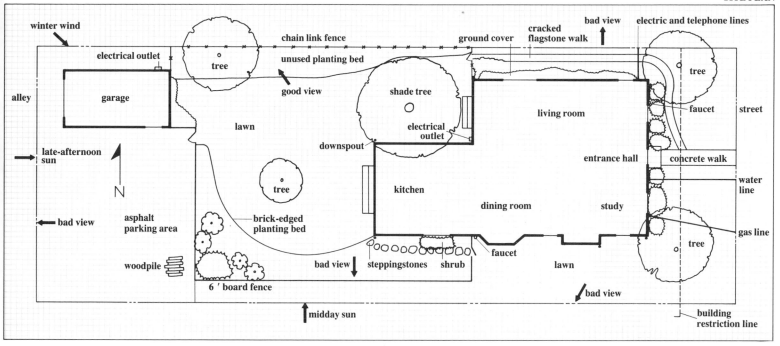

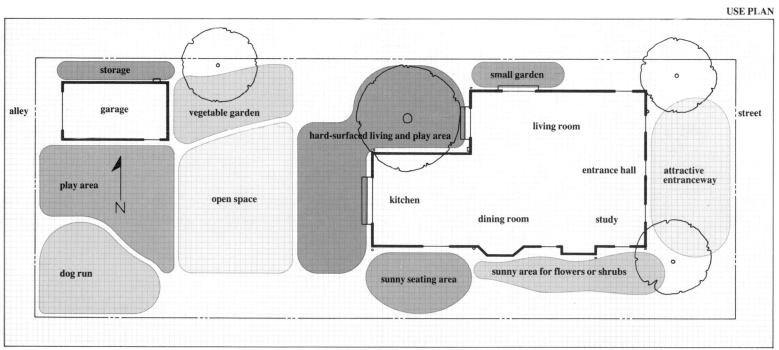

The sketches above represent two stages in designing the outdoor living space for a family with small children. The top sketch is a site plan of the existing yard, showing the boundaries of the 47-by-128-foot lot and all of its principal plants and structural features. The lower drawing is a use plan, in which roughly defined areas of the yard have been designated for different functions.

Most of the information for the site plan can be gathered in a few hours. The best tool for taking long measurements is a 100-foot cloth tape on a reel. To establish a point of reference for all the measurements, use a property line or a side of the house as a base line. Making one square on

your graph paper equal 1 foot, draw the base line on the paper so that the rest of the plan will fit onto the sheet (or, if necessary, onto two or more sheets taped together, their squares carefully aligned). Relate each measurement you take in the yard to the base line on the graph paper.

Include first-floor windows and doors, exterior faucets and electrical outlets, overhead wires and underground utility lines (so you can avoid them when digging). Utility companies can tell you where these lines are. In addition, note the position of easements that pose limitations on building. On the site plan at top, a building restriction line (*dotted line*) indicates that no permanent structure,

such as a deck, can be closer than 10 feet to public property. Finally, record information about views, wind and sunlight.

When the site plan is complete, clip an overlay of tracing paper to it and begin working out the use plan. Experiment with different arrangements, changing the tracing paper as often as necessary until you achieve the best scheme. In this case, the final plan was drawn on clean graph paper so the use areas could be easily visualized without utility lines and many existing features the planners decided to remove — including the asphalt parking area, a 6-foot fence and a tree in the middle of the backyard lawn.

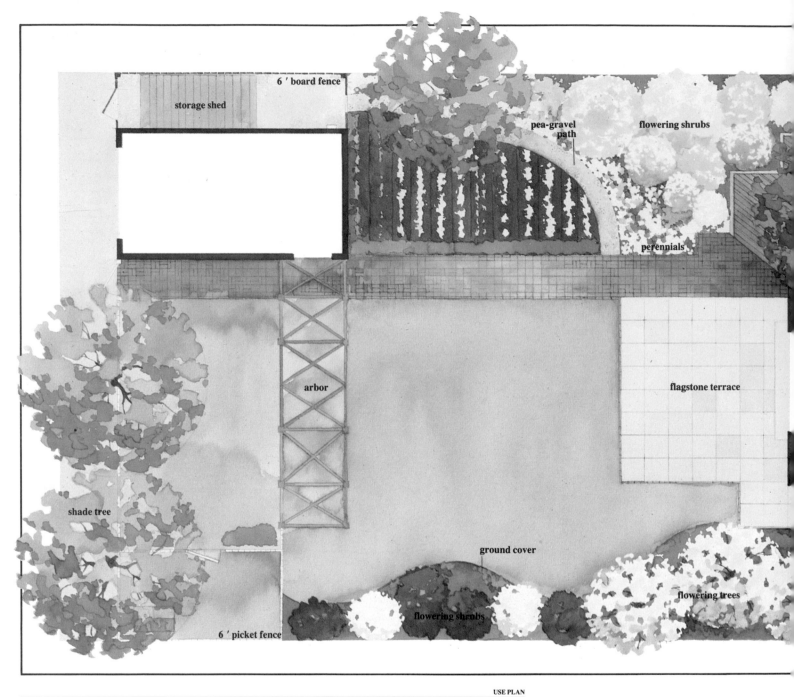

storage shed

6 ' board fence

pea-gravel
path

flowering shrubs

perennials

flagstone terrace

arbor

shade tree

ground cover

flowering trees

flowering shrubs

6 ' picket fence

USE PLAN

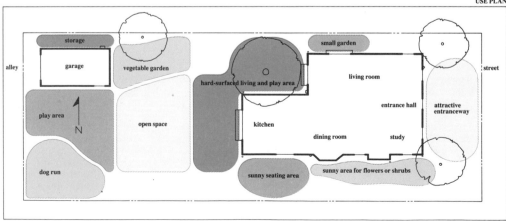

alley

storage

garage

vegetable garden

play area

open space

dog run

N

small garden

hard-surfaced living and play area

living room

entrance hall

kitchen

dining room

study

attractive
entranceway

street

sunny seating area

sunny area for flowers or shrubs

Using Rectangles to Achieve Formality

Straight lines and right angles give a look of formality to a design *(above)* that fleshes out the bare bones of the use plan *(left)*. A bold, 9-foot-wide brick walk bisects the front yard and leads to a new and larger stoop. Plantings here are low: The lawn bordering the walk gives way to shade-tolerant ground cover beneath the two trees, and dwarf evergreens that will not obscure the windows even at maturity are used to flank the stoop.

A narrow brick walk leads around the corner of the house into the north side

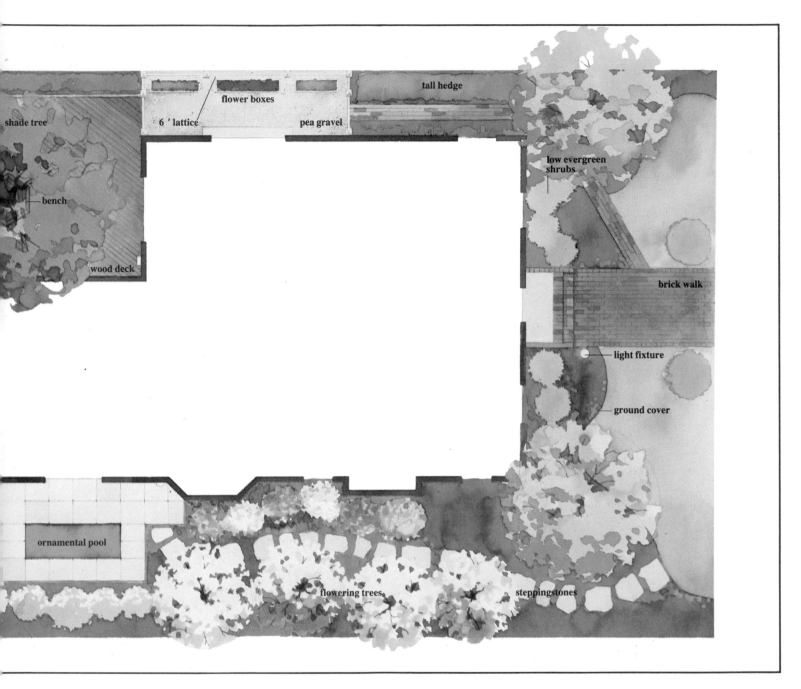

shade tree

bench

wood deck

flower boxes

6 ' lattice

pea gravel

tall hedge

low evergreen shrubs

brick walk

light fixture

ground cover

ornamental pool

flowering trees

steppingstones

yard. Part of this cramped, awkward space has been transformed into a 6-by-18-foot pocket garden that provides an attractive view from the living-room window. The little flower-box garden is backed by a 6-foot-high lattice that screens the view into the neighboring yard. At each end of the lattice, a tall hedge is kept neatly sheared, both to maintain the formal style and to keep the hedge within bounds.

On the opposite, south side of the house, small flowering trees screen the first-floor windows in summer but shed their leaves to admit winter sunshine. A flagstone terrace wraps around the kitch-

en for convenient outdoor dining. From here there is a long view across the vegetable garden and the neighbor's back lawn that gives a sense of space and makes the yard appear larger.

A change in materials underscores the different character of a second sitting area, the wood deck. This more intimate spot is sheltered by house walls, shrubbery and the large tree around which the deck and a bench are built. A brick walk provides dry footing and direct access from the garage to the house.

At the rear of the yard, a play area beyond the arbor is clearly visible from the kitchen, so children can be easily super-

vised. A 6-foot picket fence surrounding the dog run is aligned with the arbor and the garage wall to direct the eye across the yard and create an illusion of width. The fence also backs up the play area, keeping children from darting out into the path of cars in the alley, and blocks out an unattractive view.

6´ board fence

woodpile

flowering shrubs

flagstone terrace

ornamental pool

ground cover

shade tree

evergreen shrubs

USE PLAN

storage

garage

vegetable garden

small garden

hard-surfaced living and play area

living room

alley

play area

open space

kitchen

entrance hall

attractive entranceway

street

dining room

study

dog run

sunny seating area

sunny area for flowers or shrubs

N

Sinuous Curves for a Casual Look

A second design *(above)* elaborates the use plan *(left)* with curvilinear forms that fulfill all the same functions as those met by the more formal plan shown on the preceding pages. The two designs have essentially the same elements, including ample terrace and deck space, large trees to block the hot afternoon sun, a dog run and a storage area located in relatively unobtrusive spots. One important difference is that where the first design relied principally on shrubs and trees for privacy along the side boundaries, this scheme

calls for a 6-foot-high board fence on three sides of the property.

Again there is a pocket garden on the north side of the house, this time defined by a semicircular bulge in the brick walk that connects the front and back yards. Here, lattice forms a backdrop for a statue, whose small size is in scale with the dimensions of its setting. The view from inside the living room focuses on this diminutive scene.

In the backyard the brick walk widens into a terrace beneath the large shade tree. Because of the tree's protruding roots, the center of the terrace is left unpaved and is instead planted with ground cover. The walks and the two terraces — one of them flagstone — provide a lengthy run for children playing with tricycles and other wheeled toys.

On the south side of the house, a deck provides a seating area especially useful in the cool months of the year, when it will catch the sun and be partially sheltered by the house from chilly winds. Deciduous vines trained on the arbor overhead would create shade in summer to help keep the kitchen as well as the deck more comfortable.

At the rear of the yard, the concrete apron abutting the alley is slightly wider to allow easier parking parallel to the fence. This requires planting the new pair of shade trees inside the play area and the dog run, rather than beyond them as in the first design.

Outdoor furnishings

Carefully chosen outdoor furnishings can make almost any outdoor living area an enjoyable place to entertain, play or simply relax. Although naturally more rugged than their indoor counterparts, outdoor furnishings can be as tasteful, imaginative and colorful as anything you would choose for your house.

The readiest furnishings, of course, are the commercially manufactured ones; they usually require only installation, for which simple tools and techniques are adequate. The hammock swing at right, for example, is suspended between two sturdy uprights of a poolside trellis by chains attached to hooks that screw into the wood. Similar fasteners rig up a porch swing, a child's play swing, and a rope ladder *(pages 24-25)*.

With only a few more tools and hours, you can tailor benches, love seats and other accessories to suit the contours and proportions of your yard or garden. A Victorian-era bench *(pages 38-45)*, wrapped snugly around the trunk of a leafy shade tree, fits in with virtually any architectural style. Or you can build sturdy, modern 4-by-4 benches *(pages 34-37)* that can be joined together in whatever configuration suits your fancy.

Since plants are synonymous with the out-of-doors, any containers to display and transport them are always welcome additions to the yard. Even the smallest apartment terraces can be enlivened by greenery framed in handsome redwood plant boxes treated with a clear wood finish or varnish *(pages 30-33)*. To provide brilliant color accents, rows of potted plants or flowers can be conveniently arranged in an old-fashioned plant tray *(pages 26-29)* that doubles as a carryall for cuttings or freshly picked garden vegetables.

Napping comes easy on this 54-by-82-inch cotton rope hammock invitingly installed underneath a poolside trellis. The hammock hangs from heavy galvanized-steel chains attached to hooks and lag-threaded screw eyes that are fastened into the vertical beams of the trellis. The height of the hammock can be adjusted at each end by passing the hook through links at different points along the chain.

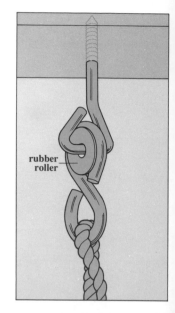

rubber
roller

A traditional wood porch swing provides a quiet setting for summer reading, relaxation — and romance. The preassembled seat, purchased unfinished and painted to match the color of the ceiling, is suspended from ⁵⁄₁₆-inch hooks screwed into the 2-by-10 joists (*drawing, right*). The joists run parallel to one another at 16-inch intervals across the ceiling or along its length and hold the ceiling up on their 2-inch-wide dimension. To find the joists, drill small holes into the ceiling and probe with a wire; any extra holes can be filled later with vinyl spackling compound. The height of the swing is fixed by adjusting the length of the galvanized-steel chains.

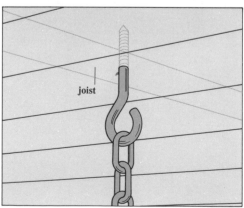

joist

Children can safely play on this flexible sling swing installed on a crossbar of a jungle gym. Eye hooks screw into the bar, and the S hooks that connect them to the rope are fitted with rubber rollers (*drawing, above*) that allow the sling to move freely without fraying the ropes. The height of the sling can be adjusted by repositioning a second pair of S-shaped hooks that secure the rope knots on each side.

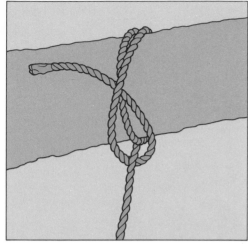

A simple rope ladder transforms a gnarled oak into a child's lookout tower. The ends of the ropes are tied around the branch with a double half hitch, as shown above. First pass the rope over the branch and loop it back under itself *(top)*, then pass the end around the rope again and loop it under itself again *(center)*. Push the two coils together and pull the knot tight *(bottom)*. When weight is applied to the ladder, the knot tightens.

A portable garden in a tray

Potted plants become a movable feast for the eyes when arrayed in a plant tray that can be transported almost effortlessly from porch to patio to potting shed. The tray shown here is 11¼ inches wide and 24 inches long — big enough to accommodate eight 5-inch plant pots, or masses of freshly picked fruits and vegetables.

In this example, the sides of the endpieces curve gently upward — a design easily duplicated with the aid of a grid *(Steps 1 and 2)*. Other designs are just as simple to copy *(page 29)* or invent. All that is required for making the tray is inexpensive lumber: pine, redwood, cedar or spruce, for example. Have the lumberyard or millwork cut the boards to the lengths specified in the Materials List *(right)*, or saw the wood yourself with a crosscut saw or a circular power saw *(pages 122-123)*.

Shaping the endpieces into the gentle curves shown here requires a saber saw; corner clamps are essential for holding joints in alignment as you nail the pieces together.

After the tray is assembled, sand it with fine (150-grit) sandpaper to smooth the flat surfaces and round the edges. Then, depending on the effect you want, you can either let the wood weather naturally, apply an outdoor stain like the one shown here, or paint the wood in your choice of colors.

Materials List

1 x 4	3 pieces clear pine 1 x 4, 24 " long	**Dowel**	1⅜ " closet-rod dowel, 24 " long
1 x 12	2 pieces clear pine 1 x 12, 16 " long	**Nails**	¼ lb. sixpenny galvanized-steel common nails
Lath	4 pieces 1⅛ " x ¼ " lath, 25½ " long		2 oz. 1 " galvanized-steel wire nails

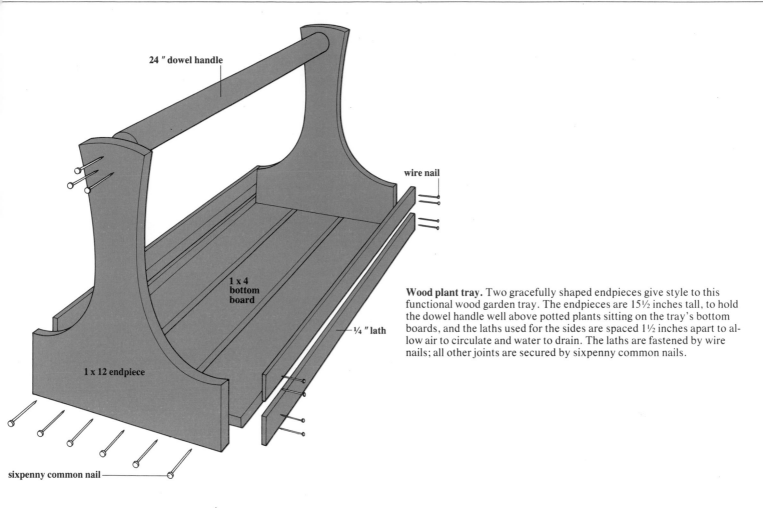

24 " dowel handle

wire nail

1 x 4 bottom board

¼ " lath

1 x 12 endpiece

sixpenny common nail

Wood plant tray. Two gracefully shaped endpieces give style to this functional wood garden tray. The endpieces are 15½ inches tall, to hold the dowel handle well above potted plants sitting on the tray's bottom boards, and the laths used for the sides are spaced 1½ inches apart to allow air to circulate and water to drain. The laths are fastened by wire nails; all other joints are secured by sixpenny common nails.

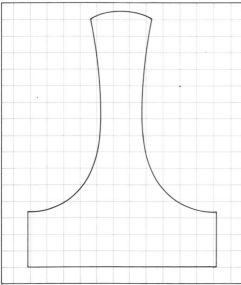

1 **Making the endpiece pattern.** Draw a grid of 1-inch squares on a 15-by-17-inch piece of lightweight cardboard or heavy paper. Then mark the points where the outline of the endpiece crosses the lines of the grid. Using the pattern above as a guide, connect the marks, then fold the cardboard or paper in half lengthwise and cut out the pattern with scissors.

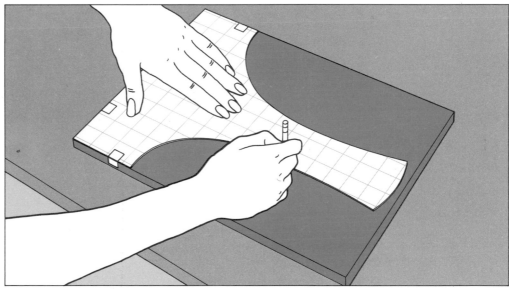

2 **Transferring the pattern to wood.** Put the endpiece pattern on a 16-inch length of 1-by-12 so that the upward sweep of the pattern runs in the same direction as the grain of the wood. Tape the base of the pattern to hold it steady. Then trace around the edge of the pattern with a pencil. In similar fashion, transfer the pattern to a second 16-inch 1-by-12. ▶

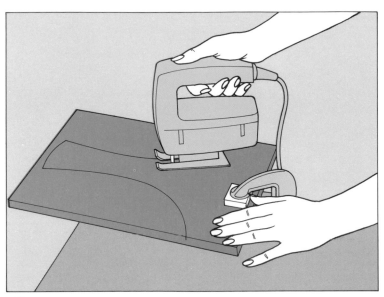

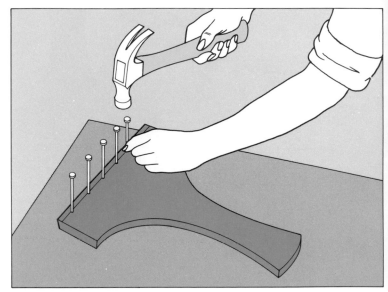

3 **Cutting out the endpiece.** Position one board on a work surface with one half of the traced pattern overhanging the edge. Clamp the board in place, fitting a piece of scrap wood between the C clamp and the board to protect the wood's surface. Cut out the overhanging piece with a saber saw; then reposition and clamp the board to cut the other half of the piece. Cut the other endpiece in the same way. Finally, smooth the curves of the endpieces with coarse (60-grit) sandpaper.

4 **Starting the nails.** On both side edges of the endpieces, make tick marks ⅜ inch from the bottom. Connect the marks with a light pencil line. Mark locations for nails along the line, 1, 3 and 5 inches from each end. Then drive a sixpenny common nail about ½ inch into the wood at each of the marks. Measure, mark and start nails in the other endpiece.

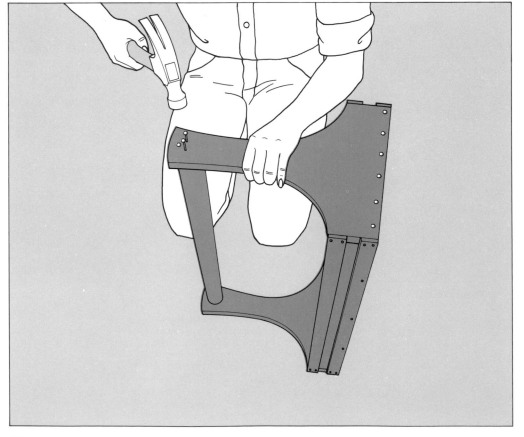

7 **Attaching the handle.** Set the tray on end and stand a 24-inch dowel between the tops of the two endpieces. Center the dowel, positioning one of its edges ¼ inch below the top of each endpiece. Nail each endpiece to the rod by driving in three sixpenny common nails ¾ inch apart in a small triangle.

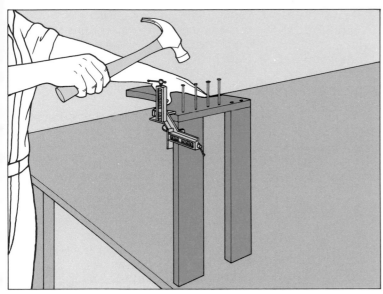

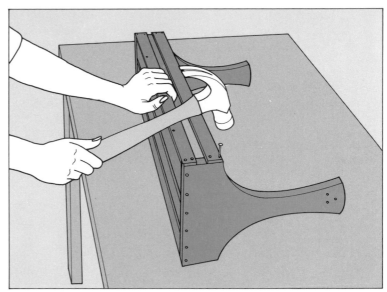

5 **Nailing the bottom slats.** Align a 24-inch 1-by-4 flush with the bottom and side edge of an endpiece. Secure the board with a corner clamp and drive in the first two nails. Align, clamp and nail another 1-by-4 to the other side of the endpiece *(above)*. Then center the third board, adjusting its spacing between the two outer boards, and nail it in place. Finally, turn the whole assembly over and nail the other endpiece to the 1-by-4s.

6 **Attaching the sides.** Lay the tray on its side and position a strip of 25½-inch lath so one long side is flush with the bottom of the tray and the ends are flush with the faces of the endpieces. Drive wire nails into each endpiece through the top and bottom edges of the lath. Then nail the lath to the adjacent bottom-board slat with wire nails, set ⅜ inch from the bottom of the lath and located 6 inches from each end and at the center. Align the top lath between the endpieces so its top edge is flush with the bottom of the endpiece curve, and nail it in place at both ends. Follow the same procedure for the lath strips on the other side of the tray.

Alternate Designs

The three endpiece patterns shown below suggest some of the ways you can vary the plant tray pictured on page 26.

All share the same basic measurements, so the materials list need not change and the construction techniques in this demonstration will apply to them.

If you wish to design your own pattern, keep the outline simple: Straight lines and gentle curves are the easiest forms to cut with a saber saw. Be sure to keep the support for the handle 3 inches wide at its narrowest point so the tray can be lifted safely. Enlarge your drawing by transferring it onto a 15-by-17-inch grid, then cut it out and trace around it onto the wood.

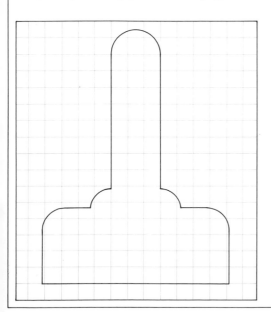

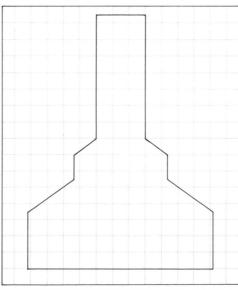

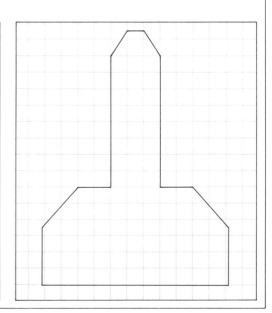

A versatile planter

Planted with flowers or a shrub, this handsome redwood box can bring the pleasant freshness of a garden to even a small balcony, courtyard or terrace. Easily assembled from 1-by-12 boards and 1-by-2 slats, the planter is capped with mitered molding around the top edge that gives it a professionally finished appearance. And the slats can be applied to the basic box in a number of patterns, allowing you to vary the design to suit your taste *(page 33)*.

Smooth-milled boards give this planter a clean, sleek look; for a more rustic appearance, buy rough-sawn lumber. Ask for clear, warp-resistant redwood heartwood. (Cut from the center portion of the tree, heartwood is less permeable and more durable than the surrounding sapwood.) You may wish to pay a little extra to have the lumber dealer cut the 1-by-12 lengths that are specified in the Materials List below, because those pieces need perfectly squared edges to butt to-

gether neatly at the corners. If you cut them yourself, use a circular saw and check that the blade is square to the faceplate before starting. You can easily saw the 1-by-2s to length yourself, and it is necessary to do so in the case of some of the alternative designs on page 33.

Once the basic cutting is done, you need only a few simple tools to construct the planter. A miter box and a backsaw (a saw with a steel-reinforced spine that keeps the blade rigid) will enable you to make the 45° cuts for mitered corners. A pair of corner clamps will hold the pieces in alignment while you nail them together (use galvanized-steel nails and brads, which will not rust). To cut drainage holes in the planter's bottom *(Step 1)*, use a power drill fitted with a ½-inch spade bit.

Smooth any splintery edges of the completed planter with coarse (60-grit) sandpaper. Although the redwood needs no protective finish — its natural acidity resists insects and rot — a clear wood finish, as shown here, or varnish will improve the planter's appearance.

Materials List	
1 x 12	5 ′ redwood 1 x 12, cut into: 3 pieces, 11¼ ″ long 2 pieces, 12⅝ ″ long
1 x 2	30 ′ redwood 1 x 2, cut into: 26 pieces, 11¼ ″ long 4 pieces, 16 ″ long
Nails	1 lb. fourpenny galvanized-steel finishing nails 2 oz. galvanized-steel brads, 1¼ ″ long

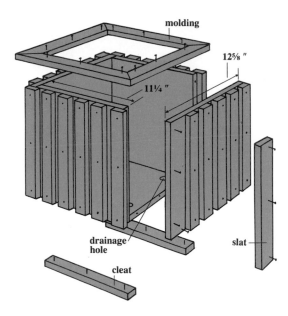

molding

12⅝ "

11¼ "

drainage hole

cleat

slat

The measure of a simple box. The planter pieces fit together because their lengths are based on the actual dimensions of nominal 1-by-12 redwood: ¹¹⁄₁₆ inch thick by 11¼ inches wide. The bottom is cut 11¼ inches long to make it square. Two side pieces of that length are nailed to the bottom's side edges; two others 12⅝ inches long overlap the ends of the shorter sides. The 11¼-inch slats match the height of the box, which is held off the ground by cleats.

1 **Drilling drainage holes.** Using a straightedge, draw two diagonal lines connecting opposite corners of one of the 11¼-inch-long 1-by-12s. Measure 4 inches from each corner along the lines and make tick marks with a pencil. Put the 1-by-12 on a piece of scrap board and bore holes at each of the marked locations with a drill fitted with a ½-inch spade bit. Then drill a hole in the center, where the diagonals intersect.

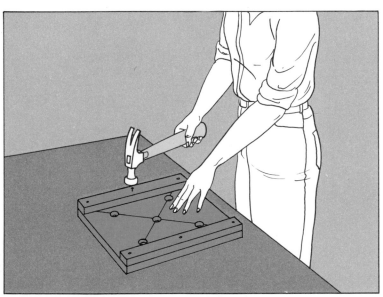

2 **Attaching the cleats.** Place two of the 11¼-inch-long 1-by-2s on the board you have just drilled, laying them lengthwise with the 1-by-12's grain and aligning them with its edges as shown above. Nail each 1-by-2 in position with three 1¼-inch galvanized-steel brads located 1 inch from each end and at the middle of the strip. The 1-by-2s serve as cleats to raise the plant box off the ground.

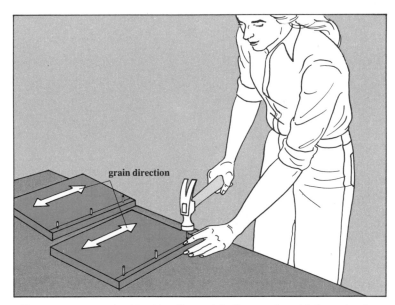

grain direction

3 **Marking the short sides.** Pencil a straight line running with the grain of an 11¼-inch-long 1-by-12, parallel to and ⅜ inch from one edge of the board. Mark nail positions on the line 1½ inches from each end and about ½ inch from the midpoint — not precisely at the midpoint because a nail there, when driven into the bottom board, might collide with a cleat nail. Then tap a fourpenny finishing nail approximately ½ inch into the wood at each of the marked locations. Mark a second 11¼-inch-long board in the same way and start nails into the marked positions. ▶

31

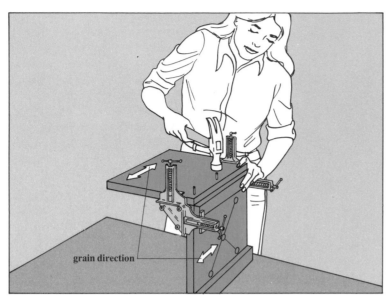

grain direction

4 **Nailing the short sides to the bottom.** With the grain of both boards running in the same direction, attach a short side piece to the bottom board with corner clamps as seen above. Align them so that the edge of the side piece is flush with the bottom surface of the bottom board and the nails are in position to be driven into the edge of the bottom board. Then drive the nails home. Now align, clamp and nail the second short side piece to the opposite edge of the bottom piece.

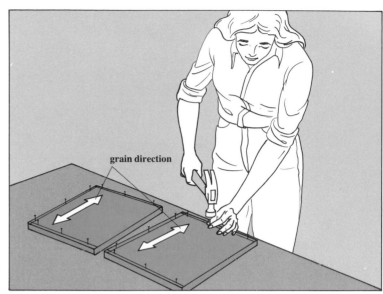

grain direction

5 **Marking the long sides.** On one of the 12⅝-inch-long side pieces, pencil a line running with the grain, ⅜ inch from and parallel to one edge. Mark nail positions on the line 1¼ inches from each end and at the midpoint. Now draw lines parallel to and ⅜ inch from the two adjacent edges, and mark three nail positions on each of those lines: Put marks 1½ inches from each end and 5½ inches from one end — not at the exact midpoint, where the nailhead might interfere with a nail that will be driven later to attach a trim slat. Drive a fourpenny finishing nail about ½ inch into the wood at each of the marked locations. Then mark the second 12⅝-inch 1-by-12 the same way and start the nails in that board.

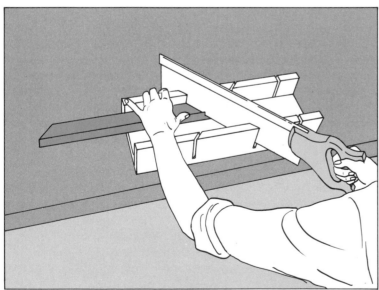

8 **Cutting the mitered molding.** Put a 16-inch 1-by-2 slat against the back of a miter box and use a backsaw to make a 45° cut approximately ½ inch from one end. Remove the slat from the miter box and lay it flat along the top edge of the plant box so that the obtuse (broad) angle of the cut end is aligned with an inside corner of the box. Then mark the other end of the slat where it touches the inside corner on that side of the box. Put the slat back into the miter box so that the obtuse angle of the cut end points away from you *(above)*; align the mark with the saw guide at the back of the miter box and cut a 45° angle at the other end. The piece will now exactly fit one edge of the plant box. Miter the ends of the three remaining slats in the same way.

9 **Attaching the molding.** Align the inside edge of a mitered piece of cap molding with an inside edge of the top of the box, and nail the molding in place with fourpenny galvanized-steel finishing nails: Place the nails ⅜ inch from the slat's inner edge at positions 1 inch from each end of the inner edge and at the midpoint. Then align and nail the remaining molding pieces to the top of the box. Use a nail set to countersink all the visible nailheads in the molding and trim slats. Fill in the nail holes with redwood-tinted wood putty. Finally, sand any rough edges smooth with coarse (60-grit) sandpaper.

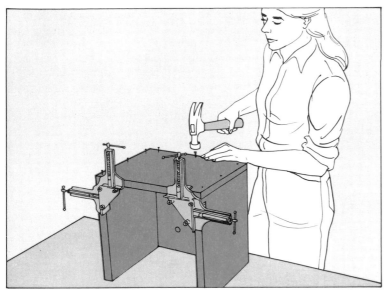

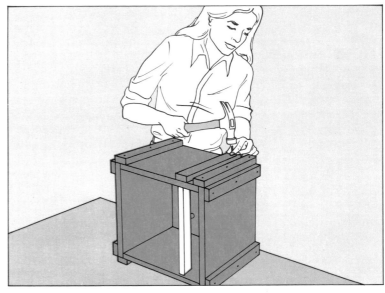

6 **Attaching the long sides.** Align the edges of one long side piece with the outer surfaces of the bottom and the short side pieces so that the nails in the long side piece are in position to be driven into the edges of the other pieces. Fasten the pieces together with corner clamps as shown above and drive in all the nails. Complete the basic box by aligning, clamping and nailing the second long piece to the other side.

7 **Attaching trim slats.** Count out eight trim slats to attach at the box's corners. On the face of each, mark three nail positions ⅜ inch from one long edge: Mark the positions 1 inch from each end of the slat and at its midpoint. Now place the box on its side and position a slat along one corner so its edge is flush with the vertical side and its nail marks are ⅜ inch from that side. Nail it in place with 1¼-inch galvanized brads. Attach the rest of the corner slats the same way. Next, wedge a slat inside the box as shown to brace the upper side while you use three brads to nail a slat about ⅝ inch from one of the corner slats. Continue around the box attaching four slats between each pair of corner slats, about ⅝ inch apart, moving the wedge to support the upper side as you go.

Planter Patterns Tailored to Taste

Once you have built the basic box out of 1-by-12s, you can attach the decorative slats in a variety of ways. Three easily assembled designs are illustrated below.

To create a close-set vertical pattern *(left)*, use a total of 32 slats, positioning them on the box's sides so they touch each other, eight on a side. The diamond pattern *(center)* consists of four slats mitered at a 45° angle at each end and approximately 8 inches long from tip to tip. Or arrange the slats diagonally *(right)*, measuring and mitering each individual piece to fit flush with the edges of the box.

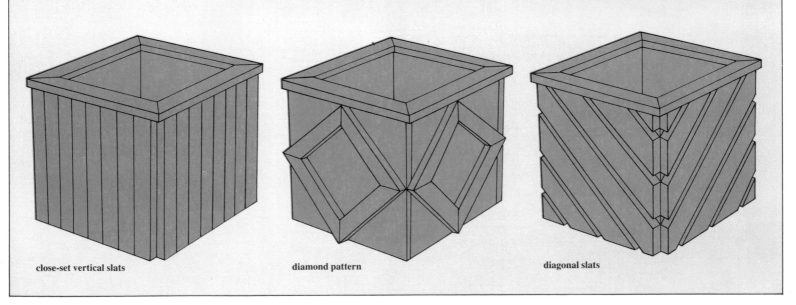

close-set vertical slats   diamond pattern   diagonal slats

Durable garden benches

Rugged outdoor benches such as those shown below will weather attractively and last a lifetime, but they are neither difficult nor time-consuming to build. Only 12 pieces of standard-sized lumber are required for a bench, and it can be put together in less than a day.

The bench is constructed of pressure-treated 4-by-4 pine timbers, which have been cut to length by the lumberyard. The pieces are held together by threaded steel rods that are secured with nuts and washers. Apart from some measuring, construction consists of little more than drilling holes for the threaded rods, cutting the rods to the proper length and assembling the components. The hardest part of the job may be moving the bench: It weighs about 75 pounds.

Only a few tools are required: a power drill, a drill guide, a socket wrench, a hacksaw, and a small flat metalworking file. You will also need ⅝-inch and 1-inch spade bits to drill holes for the rods and the recessed nuts and washers, and a pair of C clamps to secure the rods to the worktable while you cut them.

After you have assembled the bench, use coarse (60-grit) sandpaper to smooth the exposed surfaces and round off the corners, eliminating any splinters that might snag clothing or skin. You can leave the wood unfinished for a rustic look. If you wish instead to paint it, use an exterior enamel and apply it before as-

sembling the timbers; otherwise you will not be able to reach their inner surfaces with the brush.

Because of its simplicity, this bench invites duplication. If you make more than one, you can arrange them to suit your backyard. Line them up end to end to delineate boundaries of a patio or garden. Two benches placed perpendicular to each other form a corner nook; side by side they create a broad seating or sunning platform.

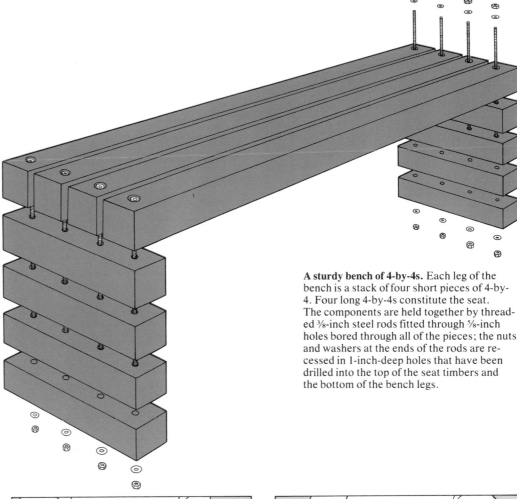

A sturdy bench of 4-by-4s. Each leg of the bench is a stack of four short pieces of 4-by-4. Four long 4-by-4s constitute the seat. The components are held together by threaded ⅜-inch steel rods fitted through ⅝-inch holes bored through all of the pieces; the nuts and washers at the ends of the rods are recessed in 1-inch-deep holes that have been drilled into the top of the seat timbers and the bottom of the bench legs.

Materials List (for one bench)	
Lumber	36 ′ pressure-treated pine 4 x 4, cut into: 4 pieces, 6 ′ long 8 pieces, 17 ″ long
Steel rod	4 pieces ⅜ ″ threaded galvanized-steel rod, 3 ′ long
Nuts and washers	16 galvanized-steel ⅜ ″ nuts 16 galvanized-steel ⅜ ″ washers

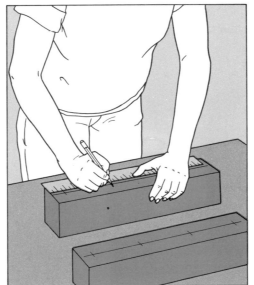

1 **Marking hole locations.** Measure the width of one surface of each 17-inch 4-by-4 and use a straightedge to draw a lengthwise line down its center. Then measure 1¾ and 6¾ inches from each end, and mark those positions on the center line of each piece. Next, locate the center of the width of each 6-foot 4-by-4, and mark it at 1¾ inches from each end.

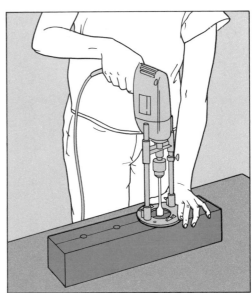

2 **Counterboring holes for the nuts.** Using a drill fitted with a 1-inch spade bit and a drill guide adjusted to bore to a depth of 1 inch, drill at the marked locations on only two of the 17-inch 4-by-4s; these 1-inch-deep holes will serve as recesses for the nuts on the bottoms of the legs. Then drill the same size of hole at each of the marked locations on all the 6-foot 4-by-4s, to provide recesses in the bench's top surface. ▶

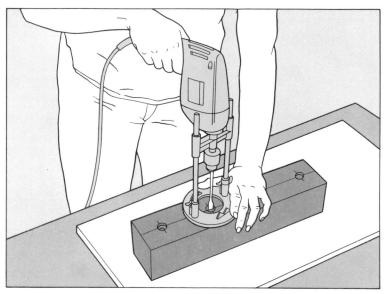

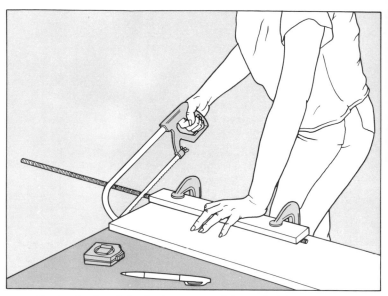

3 **Drilling holes for threaded rods.** Equip the drill with a ⅝-inch spade bit. Place one of the counterbored 4-by-4s on a piece of scrap board and adjust the drill guide so the bit will bore completely through the 4-by-4 and into, but not through, the scrap. Position the tip of the bit in the middle of a counterbored hole, then drill through the 4-by-4. Drill similar ⅝-inch holes through all of the 4-by-4s, at the counterbored holes and at all the other marked locations.

4 **Cutting the threaded rods.** At a corner of the worktable, clamp one 3-foot threaded rod tightly between two scrap boards, letting almost 2 feet of the rod extend beyond the boards and table. Measure 17½ inches from the overhanging end, and cut the rod there with a hacksaw fitted with a blade for cutting mild steel. Unclamp the remaining length of rod, measure 17½ inches from the uncut end and mark the spot. Clamp the rod to the table again and cut it at the mark. Smooth the newly cut ends of the two 17½-inch lengths with a flat file, holding the file at an angle to bevel the ends of the rods. Then fit a ⅜-inch washer and nut onto one end of each piece. Measure and cut the remaining three rods and fit them with washers and nuts in the same way.

6 **Mounting the seat timbers.** Turn the two assembled bench legs on their sides, as seen at left, and slip a 6-foot 4-by-4 onto the two lowest protruding rods. Put a washer and nut on each rod and tighten the nuts by hand. Mount the remaining three 4-by-4s the same way. Finally, tighten all of the nuts with a %₁₆-inch socket wrench, using another socket wrench, or jamming a large screwdriver into the hole at the other end of each rod, to keep the bottom nuts from turning.

5 **Assembling the bench legs.** Place one of the counterbored 17-inch 4-by-4s on the worktable with its holes parallel to the tabletop. Slide threaded rods through the holes at the ends of the timber, pushing the rods until the washers and nuts are inside the counterbored holes. Then slide three of the 17-inch 4-by-4s that were not counterbored onto the protruding rods; the ends of the rods will extend about 4 inches beyond the four timbers. Now insert rods into the two inner counterbored holes and slide them through. Follow the same procedure to insert rods into the remaining four 17-inch 4-by-4s to assemble the other bench leg.

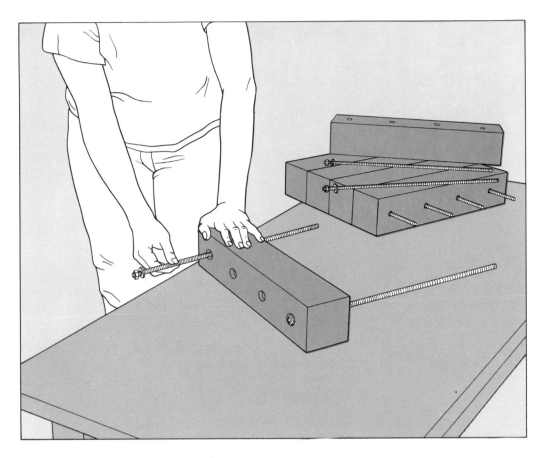

7 **Aligning the bench.** Set the bench upright and examine it to see if the seat timbers are evenly spaced. To adjust the spacing between timbers, loosen the nuts with the socket wrench and use a large screwdriver as a lever to move the 4-by-4s from side to side. When the spacing is even at both ends of the bench, tighten the nuts again.

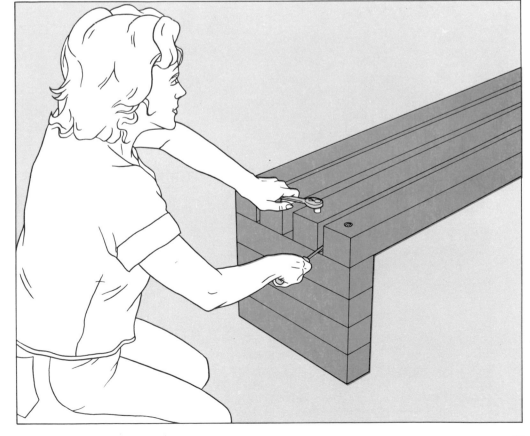

The classic charm of a tree bench

Outdoor furniture should be pleasing to the eye as well as functional; the around-the-tree bench at left satisfies both requirements — with panache. It can seat half a dozen people, hold potted plants or cutting baskets, even serve as a low picnic table. And its geometric design — six wedge-shaped sections joined together to form a hexagon — blends gracefully into almost any architectural setting.

The bench is designed so most of its components can easily be cut with a circular saw from pieces precut to prescribed lengths (Materials List, below). For example, all the pieces in each wedge have angled ends, but the angle in every case is 60°, so the cuts can be made accurately with the aid of a simple homemade jig (pages 40-41, Steps 1-3). To obtain the 2-inch-thick supports for the seat boards

however, you must cut 2-by-4s lengthwise with a circular saw (a nominal 2-by-2 will not do the job because it is actually only 1½ inches thick). Lengthwise cutting, called ripping, is facilitated by inserting a wedge-shaped wood scrap or a tool called a kerf splitter into each cut (or kerf) to keep the saw blade from binding. Some lumberyards will do this kind of cutting for you at an additional charge.

The bench is made of pressure-treated yellow pine. Because this material contains chemicals that irritate eyes and lungs, always wear a face mask and goggles when sawing. Redwood, cedar, fir and untreated pine can be used if coated with a wood preservative; paint alone will not protect them from insects and rot.

The bench shown here fits a tree about 1 foot in diameter. To expand the bench's dimensions, first measure your tree's circumference; divide by 3.14 (pi) to obtain the diameter, and halve that figure to find the radius. Add 1 inch to the length of each seat board, trim piece and faceplate for every inch of radius over 6 inches.

Besides standard tools, you need a sliding T bevel to reproduce the 60° angle, a line level (Step 13) and wood stakes to level the bench around the tree, and two large (5-inch-wide) C clamps to hold the bench together during final assembly.

Since pressure-treated wood resists decay, you can leave the bench unpainted, or you can sand it and finish it with exterior paint. In either case, treat the sawed ends of the legs with wood preservative. If desired, install flagstones under the legs for a firmer footing. Complete the job by sprinkling pine chips around the base of the bench to add a decorative touch and retard the growth of grass and weeds.

Materials List

2 x 6	6 pieces pressure-treated pine 2 x 6, 6 ′ long
2 x 4	42 ′ pressure-treated pine 2 x 4, cut into: 6 pieces, 24 ″ long 6 pieces, 43 ″ long 1 piece, 72 ″ long
1 x 4	3 pieces pressure-treated pine 1 x 4, 6 ′ long
4 x 4	2 pieces pressure-treated pine 4 x 4, 5 ′ long
Hardware	2 lbs. tenpenny galvanized-steel common nails 1 lb. tenpenny galvanized-steel finishing nails 6 galvanized-steel post caps for 4 x 4s

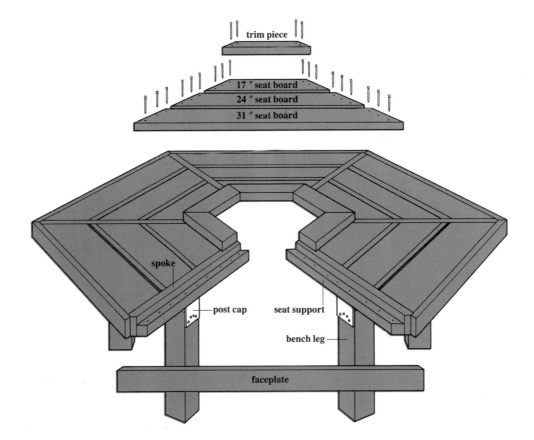

Wrap-around tree bench. This outdoor bench consists of six pie-shaped wedges that form a broad hexagon around a tree. Each wedge is made of seven pieces: three seat boards, two supports, a trim piece and a faceplate. All the pieces have diagonally sawed ends, whose accurate alignment is ensured by using a plywood jig to guide the saw. The wedges are constructed separately, then joined with 2-by-4 spokes to form two bench halves; the halves are then brought to the tree and clamped together for final assembly. The seat boards, trim pieces and faceplates are fastened with tenpenny galvanized-steel finishing nails; all other joints are secured with tenpenny galvanized-steel common nails.

1 **Marking the jig.** To prepare a jig for making angled cuts, you will need a piece of plywood 9 inches wide and 30 inches long. Pencil a tick mark on one long edge, 10 inches from the right-hand end. Position a protractor on the face of the plywood so the center line on its bottom meets the tick mark. Make a mark on the face of the plywood 60° on the protractor's right-hand scale. Align a straightedge with the two marks and connect them with a line drawn across the width of the plywood.

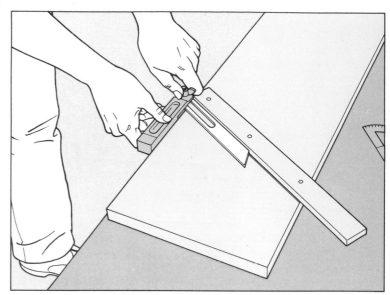

2 **Setting the T bevel.** Position a 1-foot piece of ¼-inch lath on the plywood with one edge along the far side of the angled line, then nail the lath in place with three 1-inch wire nails. Using the edge of the lath as a guide, set and lock a sliding T bevel to an angle of 60°. Check the angle you have set in the T bevel with a protractor.

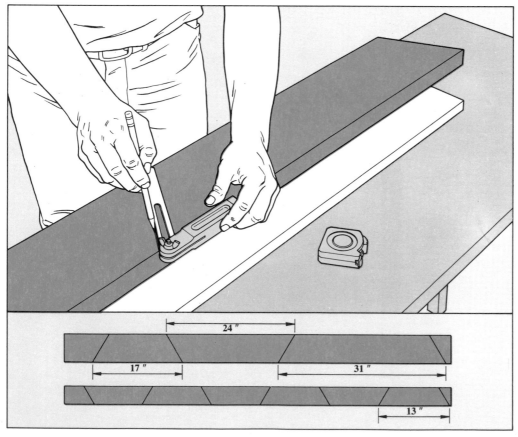

5 **Cutting seat boards.** Turn the 2-by-6 end for end. Along its far edge, measure 31 inches from the tip of the acute (sharp) angle and make a mark. Set the joint of the T bevel to the left of the mark, then draw a line across the 2-by-6 *(left)*. Reassemble the sandwich — scrap wood, 2-by-6 and jig — and saw along the line to cut out a 31-inch board.

Using the top diagram in the inset as a guide, cut the rest of the 2-by-6 into one 24-inch and one 17-inch seat board. Cut the other five 2-by-6s similarly.

Following the bottom diagram in the inset and using the same sawing techniques, cut the 6-foot 2-by-4 into six trim pieces.

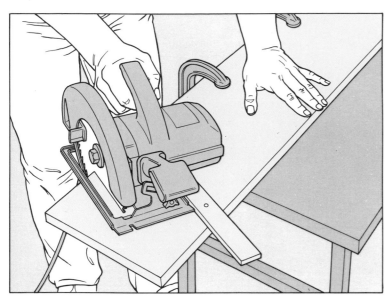

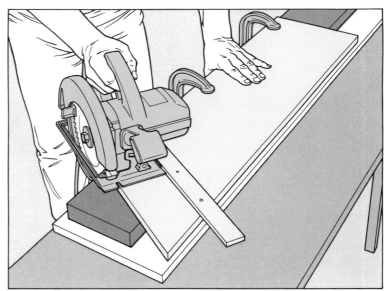

3 **Cutting the jig.** Position the jig so it overhangs the edge of the worktable. Use a C clamp to hold the piece of plywood steady. Align the base plate of a circular saw with the near edge of the angled lath; then, using the lath as a guide, cut the plywood.

4 **Making angled cuts.** On the worktable, place one 6-foot 2-by-6 over a wide piece of scrap wood at least 4 feet long, and set the jig on top of the 2-by-6 at the right-hand end. Let the end of the 2-by-6 protrude just beyond the jig's angled end. Adjust the depth of the saw blade so it will cut into, but not through, the scrap. Clamp the sandwich to the table, align the saw with the lath, and cut the 2-by-6. Remove the clamps and jig.

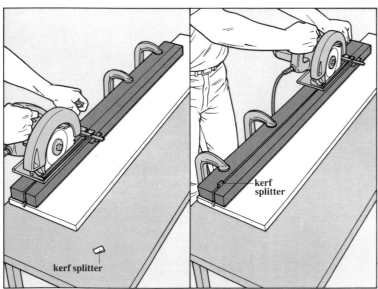

kerf splitter

kerf splitter

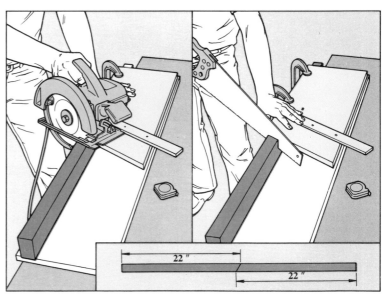

22"

22"

6 **Ripping seat supports.** To form seat supports precisely 2 inches wide and 22 inches long, first mark each 43-inch 2-by-4 with a straight penciled line 2 inches from one long edge. Put the 2-by-4 on top of the scrap wood and secure it to the worktable with two C clamps. Adjust the saw's edge guide so that the blade cuts just outside the pencil line, and cut into the board for about 10 inches. Stop the saw, push the narrow end of a kerf splitter into the cut and continue sawing until the blade nears the first C clamp. Stop the saw again, transfer both clamps to the other end of the 2-by-4, then finish the cut *(above, right)*. Save the 2-inch-wide piece for the seat support. Cut the other seat supports the same way.

7 **Cutting angled ends on seat supports.** Set one 2-inch-wide seat support on its narrow edge on top of the scrap wood. Measure 22 inches from the left end of the ripped board and make a tick mark on its far edge. Using the T bevel, draw a line across the board from the mark angling toward the left end. Sandwich the board between the scrap wood and the jig, clamp the assembly to the table, and cut the board along the line you have drawn *(above, left)*. The circular saw may not cut all the way through the board; finish the cut with a handsaw *(above, right)*. Measure, mark and cut the remaining five ripped 2-by-4s similarly. ▶

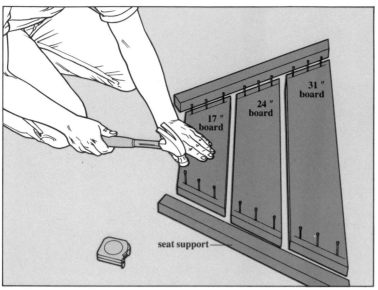

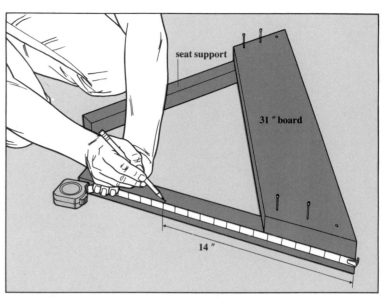

8 **Aligning the wedge-shaped bench sections.** Lay out the five pieces that constitute the first bench section — three seat boards and two seat supports — in approximate alignment. Using a straightedge, pencil a line ¾ inches from the cut ends of each seat board. Then drive three tenpenny finishing nails into, but not through, both ends of each seat board, spacing the nails 2 inches apart along the pencil lines.

9 **Nailing the outer seat boards.** Position the 31-inch seat board on top of the seat supports. Align the acute angles of the seat board with those of the supports and drive in the outermost nail on each side. Measure 14 inches from the acute angle along the outside edge of each support and make a mark. Then put the 17-inch seat board on the supports with the acute angles just touching the marks; drive in the two outermost nails.

12 **Mounting post caps.** With the bench halves still upside down, make a mark 15 inches from the inside end of one center spoke. Align the outside edge of a post cap on the mark, with its open ends facing lengthwise along the spoke, and nail it to the seat supports and 2-by-4 with tenpenny common nails. Then nail post caps to the other center spokes similarly. Attach the last two post caps to the single seat support and 2-by-4 spoke on the left-hand side of each bench half.

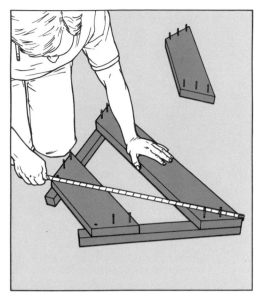

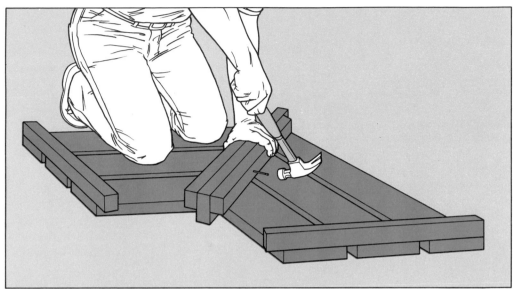

10 **Squaring the frame.** Measure diagonally across the wedge from the tip of each acute angle of the 31-inch board to the tip of the cater-cornered obtuse (broad) angle of the 17-inch board. Adjust the supports so the measured diagonals are equal. Then put the 24-inch seat board between the other two, centering it so the gaps on either side of the board are equal. Drive in all the nails. Assemble the remaining five wedges similarly.

11 **Joining the wedges.** Turn two wedge-shaped sections upside down on the floor and lay a spoke — a 24-inch-long 2-by-4 set on edge — between them so one of its ends is flush with the two inside ends of the seat supports. Kneel on one section at a time and, holding the other firmly against it, drive four tenpenny nails — spaced at equal intervals — through the side of each seat support into the spoke. Join another wedge-shaped section to one end of the assembly following the same procedure; then nail a spoke to the seat support at the left-hand end of the assembly. Join the remaining three wedges with spokes to make the other bench half.

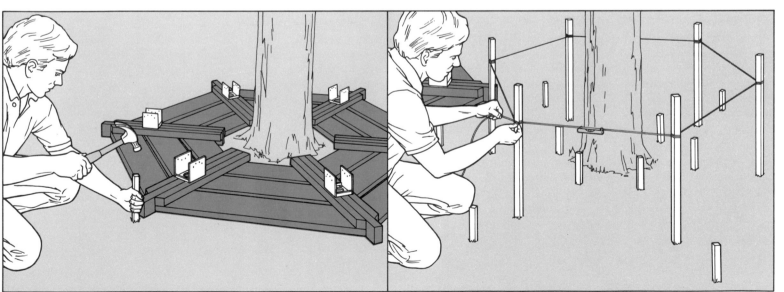

13 **Planning bench legs.** Position the two bench halves around the tree. With a hammer, drive a 6-inch wood stake into the ground at both ends of each spoke *(above, left)*. Remove the bench halves. On a line between each pair of inner and outer stakes, drive in an 18-inch stake 15 inches from the inner stake — leaving at least 16 inches of the long stake aboveground. The long stakes mark the positions of the bench legs. To determine the length of the legs, first pick a long stake that is midway between the ground's highest and lowest points, and tie a string to it 14½ inches above the ground. Stretch the string to the next stake, tie it loosely and suspend a line level from its midpoint; tighten the string when the bubble in the level's indicator is centered *(above, right)*. Now level the string around the remaining stakes. Measure the distance from the ground to the string at each stake, and mark that figure on the stake and the corresponding post cap. ▶

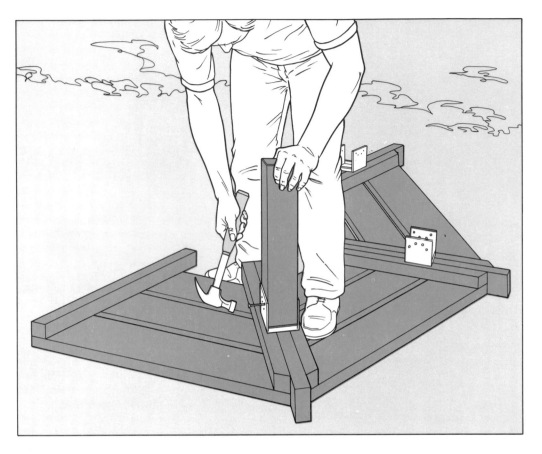

14 **Attaching the bench legs.** Saw six 4-by-4 bench legs to the lengths determined in Step 13; mark the length of each leg end so you can match it to the corresponding post cap. Brush a coat of wood preservative on the cut surfaces of the bench legs and let it dry, following the manufacturer's instructions. Then attach bench legs to the four completely attached post caps by driving tenpenny nails through the holes in the post caps *(left)*.

16 **Attaching the trim pieces.** Set the six trim pieces around the inside edge of the bench seat. Mark the outside edge of each piece on the seat board below it to ensure proper alignment. Then attach the trim pieces to the seat boards and spokes with tenpenny finishing nails. Nail the trim pieces themselves together by driving finishing nails through the angled tip of each piece into the adjoining piece.

17 **Cutting the spoke ends.** Use a straightedge and pencil to extend the angles formed by the edges of the seat boards across the top edge of each spoke *(inset)*. Then, using the lines you have drawn and the edges of the seat boards as a guide, cut off the square ends of the spokes with a handsaw. Determine the length of each faceplate for the bench by measuring the distance between spoke tips on each bench face. Record the measurements on the front edge of the corresponding seat boards.

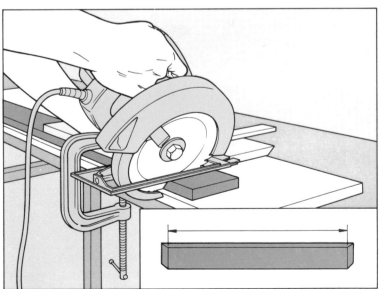

15 **Assembling the bench.** Remove all of the stakes from the site. Set the bench halves in place around the tree, then crawl under the bench to clamp the seat supports and spokes together at the joints with 5-inch C clamps. Nail the joints *(Step 11)* and the last two post caps and bench legs *(Steps 12 and 14).*

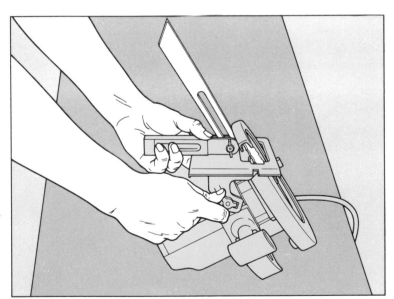

18 **Cutting the beveling jig.** To make a new jig for beveling the faceplate boards, reset the circular-saw blade to cut at an angle of 60° from the vertical. To do this, first loosen the base-plate adjustment nut on the side of the saw; then hold the sliding T bevel against the blade and move the saw's base plate until the angle between the base plate and the blade matches that of the T bevel *(above).* Retighten the adjustment nut. Now nail a piece of ¼-inch lath perpendicular to the long edge of your old jig and about 5 inches from the uncut end. Clamp the jig to the worktable and, using the lath as a guide, saw a beveled edge across the jig.

19 **Beveling the faceplates.** Put a 6-foot 1-by-4 on scrap wood, and clamp the jig on top so the 1-by-4 protrudes just beyond the jig's beveled end. Cut the board, turn it end for end and — starting from the obtuse (broad) angle of the cut — measure off the distance between the spokes *(Step 17)* and make a mark. Set the T bevel on the mark, and draw a 60° diagonal line across the board's edge. Then draw a perpendicular line across the face of the 1-by-4; clamp the board under the jig, and bevel it along the line. The cut piece *(inset)* will just fit the bench face. Measure and bevel five more faceplates from the remaining lengths of 1-by-4. Nail the faceplates to the bench with tenpenny finishing nails every 6 inches.

Dramatic effects

The visual pleasures of a garden need not be suspended when the sun goes down. Modern, low-voltage lighting systems like those shown here and on the following pages can create a dramatic chiaroscuro of light and shadow, revealing some areas, concealing others. Relatively few outdoor areas, such as front doorways and garage entrances, require the strong illumination provided by standard 120-volt lamps and fixtures. Low-cost, low-voltage lighting systems are ideal for most other purposes: enhancing home security, guiding the footsteps of visitors, and making small gardens seem spacious or large ones cozy.

Low-voltage systems are available in kit form where lighting or electrical supplies are sold, or you can buy the components separately. A typical kit consists of a power transformer that plugs into three-prong outdoor receptacles and converts standard 120-volt household current to 12 volts; a set of half a dozen outdoor fixtures fitted with either incandescent bulbs or fluorescent tubes; and lengths of single- or double-insulated electrical wire. Some kits also include a timer that automatically turns the lights on and off at preset intervals.

When planning your system, avoid overlighting, especially in small yards or gardens; use lighting to show what is important in a setting, allowing less interesting features to fall into shadow. Choose locations that hide fixtures and the glare they produce; it is the lamp's glow that should be seen rather than the lamp itself. The examples on the following pages illustrate many of the techniques you can employ to accent special plantings and landscaping by careful placement of fixtures.

Low-voltage systems can be safely installed even by people inexperienced with electrical wiring. The cables are buried in shallow trenches and do not require conduits; in most cases no special permits are needed. However, some basic safety precautions must be observed when working with any type of electrical wiring. Loose connections at the fixtures or too many fixtures on a cable can generate heat and possibly cause fire; follow the manufacturer's instructions carefully at each step of the process. Always turn off the main power to the circuit you are working on, and verify that it is off with a voltage tester. Never install fixtures closer than 8 feet from the edge of a swimming pool, and always wear rubber-soled shoes and rubber gloves when working with electrical components and wiring around any kind of water or moisture.

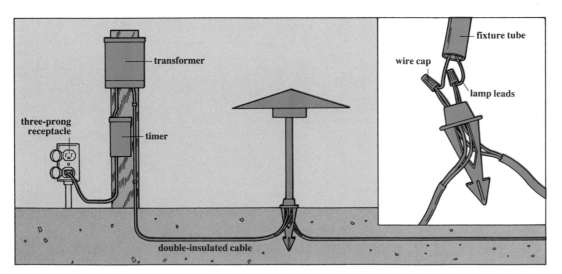

A model low-voltage system. Setting up a low-voltage lighting system usually begins with the installation of the transformer and optional timer at least 12 inches above the ground on a sturdy post or along the wall of the house; the transformer is mounted above the timer to simplify the wiring. The fixtures are attached to the transformer by means of insulated electrical cables buried in trenches 2 or 3 inches deep. At each fixture location, the insulation must be stripped off to expose the bare wires; the wire leads of the fixture lamp, similarly stripped, are then twisted around the cable's wires and secured with plastic wire caps (inset). Single-insulated cable should be pushed up into the fixture tube until the bare wires are completely isolated from the ground and safe from moisture; double-insulated cable may remain exposed outside the fixture, as shown at left.

Lighting a poolside path. Subtly placed
lamps bring out color and form in the garden
at left. As the drawing above reveals,
mushroom-shaped standing fixtures and
bullet-shaped spotlights along the path
and pool provide enough illumination — here
shown as cones of light — to guide footsteps around hazards without destroying the
mood. Additional spotlights beneath the
trees project upward to accent the foliage.

Highlighting a garden ornament. A small spotlight suspended from the branch of a maple creates a focal point as it shines down on a Japanese stone lantern. Two hidden floodlights installed near the ground illuminate either side of the lantern, thus softening the flat overhead lighting by filling in the shadows; this technique, borrowed from theater lighting and called crosslighting, imparts depth and dimension. Two additional floodlights, set behind and to either side of the lantern, throw light on the wall to silhouette the trees and other plants. Another spot, just outside the area shown, limns a tracery of shadows on the wall.

Creating drama around a pond. The tropical glamor of the garden and pond above is accentuated with skillful lighting. Two high-intensity spotlights mounted on swivel heads *(left)* partially illuminate the waterfall; similar fixtures mounted on spikes *(center)* brighten the steps leading to the house. Banks of low-voltage spotlights, arranged at different levels behind shrubbery *(far left, left and center)*, emphasize foliage and flowers, while another set of low-voltage lights *(far right)* directs its radiance toward greenery on the opposite side of the pond. Two spotlights, mounted on spikes *(far right)*, shine on the large stones along the edge of the pond, as well as on those forming a walkway in the water.

Special effects with shadows. A tree stands out in light and shadow *(right)*, illuminated by three floodlight fixtures installed behind shrubbery in a semicircle around the base of the trunk. Two additional floodlights, positioned outside the area depicted, cast diffuse light upward, providing accent illumination for leaves and branches.

Outdoor floors

Outdoors as well as inside your house, the decorative impact of the surface underfoot can be every bit as important as its utilitarian function. Brick — which can be laid in any number of patterns — lends color and an easy charm to a terrace *(pages 52-59)*. Wood gives a deck *(pages 62-75)* a casual, contemporary warmth. And flagstones *(page 61)* impart an inviting, rustic look to a garden path.

With the help of the instructions on the following pages, you can add such enhancements to your own yard or garden. But before starting, you must prepare your site carefully. As the first step, draw a complete plan. It should take into account any property lines and such impediments as steps or trees; a terrace built too close to a tree may buckle when the roots expand. Your plan should include the location of all underground water lines, gas mains and electric cables. You will not want to disrupt thcm in any way. If you are uncertain about where these lie, check with your local utility companies.

Once you have completed the plan, your next step is to stake out the site and make sure that its surface is at the proper grade. A walkway, of course, can be on level ground or follow gentle contours of the earth. But for a terrace, the land should slope ⅛ to ¼ inch per foot so that water will run off, and if the terrace is next to the house, the slope must be away from the building. The ground around most new homes is usually graded correctly and thus may need only minor adjusting. If your property has steep inclines or irregular contours, however, you must either grade the site yourself or hire a landscaper or a contractor to do it for you.

To plan the grading yourself, drive wood stakes into the ground at the four corners of the site. Tie a string around one of the stakes at what is to be the higher end of the terrace. Stretch the string to the nearest stake on the proposed downslope side of the site and tie it there. Use a line level to level the string. Allowing ¼ inch for each foot of string *(below),* use a pencil to mark the desired measurement below the knot on the downslope stake. Remove the line level, untie the string from the downslope stake and retie it at the pencil mark. (If the contour of the ground does not permit you to do this, set the string higher on both stakes, level it again and make your mark.) The string's slant represents the proper grade. Repeat these steps on the opposite side of the site. The strings can then be used as a guide for grading the surface.

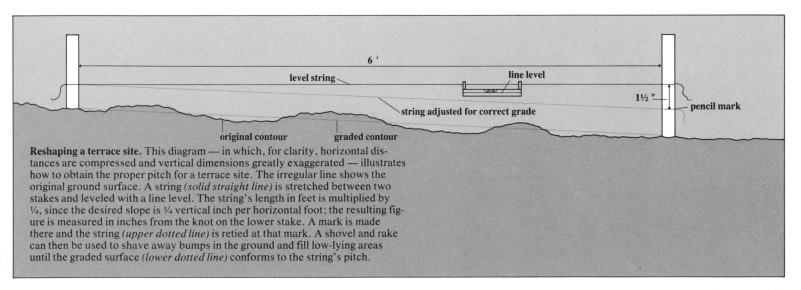

Reshaping a terrace site. This diagram — in which, for clarity, horizontal distances are compressed and vertical dimensions greatly exaggerated — illustrates how to obtain the proper pitch for a terrace site. The irregular line shows the original ground surface. A string *(solid straight line)* is stretched between two stakes and leveled with a line level. The string's length in feet is multiplied by ¼, since the desired slope is ¼ vertical inch per horizontal foot; the resulting figure is measured in inches from the knot on the lower stake. A mark is made there and the string *(upper dotted line)* is retied at that mark. A shovel and rake can then be used to shave away bumps in the ground and fill low-lying areas until the graded surface *(lower dotted line)* conforms to the string's pitch.

A terrace from bricks and sand

The rich, earthy colors and graceful lines of this brick terrace lend a rustic yet refined air to an ordinary backyard. But its virtues do not stop with charm: A brick patio enhances the value of a home without being costly or difficult to install.

The easiest brick terrace to build uses sand as a cushioning base and as filler between bricks. Here, a small amount of mortar holds the edging bricks that frame the surface. But most of the bricks rest on roofing felt atop sand, which makes laying them really quite simple.

First, prepare a sketch of your proposed patio on graph paper, taking into account any trees or other permanent features that will influence the design. Decide where you want raised edgings and where you want a so-called mowing edge, an edging flush with the ground to facilitate lawn mowing.

The terrace should slope away from the house at ⅛ to ¼ vertical inch per horizontal foot so water will drain off. Check the site's gradient by the method described on page 51; if necessary, follow the instructions there for grading the earth.

A sand-based terrace requires a stable edging so bricks will not shift. The most

common edging is wood boards — cedar, redwood and pressure-treated pine are all decay-resistant — nailed to short stakes that hold them in place. To create a brick edging, you need a temporary form to hold the bricks in place while the mortar sets. Here, 2-by-4s are used for the form's straight sections; curved sections are made of ³⁄₈-inch flexible hardboard. Have the lumberyard cut the hardboard into 3½-inch-wide strips. To fasten the form boards to stakes, use sixteenpenny duplex nails, which have a flange, or shoulder, below the nailhead. The flange stops at the wood surface and leaves the nailhead protruding, making the nails easy to extract when you dismantle the form.

The most convenient mortar to use is a dry premixed kind, available at building-supply stores. Allow one 60-pound bag for every 20 bricks you expect to use. When working with mortar, protect your hands by wearing leather-palmed work gloves. Mix only a small batch at a time to minimize waste. If the mortar begins to dry before you have used it, add a small amount of water to make it pliable again.

Paving bricks are just over 2 inches thick, and the sand bed on which they rest should be at least 2 inches deep. Thus the site must be excavated to a depth of about 4 inches (Step 1) — a sizable chore that you may wish to hire someone to do. Where severe winters cause the ground to freeze, dig 2 inches deeper and put a 2-inch layer of gravel under the sand. The gravel will aid drainage and help prevent the bricks from heaving.

You will need coarse sand for the bed and a smaller amount of fine sand to fill the crevices between bricks. Both can be purchased from masonry suppliers. For a terrace measuring 100 square feet, about 18 cubic feet of coarse sand is needed for a 2-inch-deep bed. Buy a roll of 15-pound asphaltic roofing felt to spread on top of the sand (Step 16); it will stop weeds from growing up between the bricks.

An intricate pattern like the herring-bone design here requires the cutting of more bricks than does a simple running-bond design (page 60). Buy paving bricks rated SW, for severe weathering. Calculate five bricks per square foot for bricks laid on their broad sides. This will allow for some waste in cutting. To cut the bricks, use a masonry chisel known as a brickset and a circular saw equipped with a carbide masonry blade.

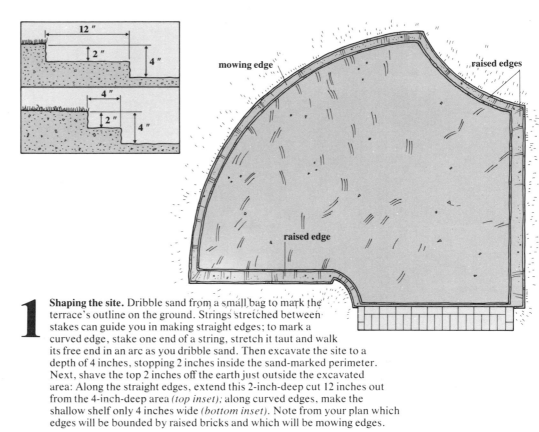

1 **Shaping the site.** Dribble sand from a small bag to mark the terrace's outline on the ground. Strings stretched between stakes can guide you in making straight edges; to mark a curved edge, stake one end of a string, stretch it taut and walk its free end in an arc as you dribble sand. Then excavate the site to a depth of 4 inches, stopping 2 inches inside the sand-marked perimeter. Next, shave the top 2 inches off the earth just outside the excavated area: Along the straight edges, extend this 2-inch-deep cut 12 inches out from the 4-inch-deep area (top inset); along curved edges, make the shallow shelf only 4 inches wide (bottom inset). Note from your plan which edges will be bounded by raised bricks and which will be mowing edges.

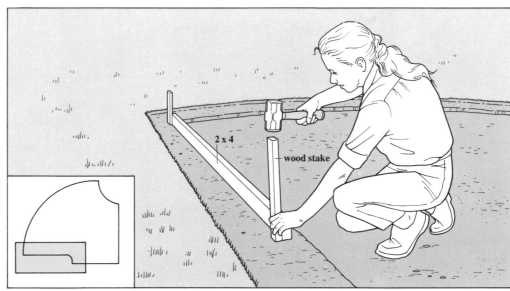

2 **Preparing a form section at a straight, raised edge.** On a straight side of the site where raised edging bricks will be used — in this case, the area indicated in the inset — set a straight 2-by-4 on edge on the 12-inch-wide shelf dug in Step 1. Position the board so its inner face is 2 inches back from the shelf's lip — just where the sand perimeter line was before it was dug away. Holding the 2-by-4 in place, use a sledge hammer to drive stakes into the ground behind it, against its outer face, at both ends of the board and at 3-foot intervals in between. ▶

3 **Nailing the form board in place.** Tap two duplex nails partway into the outer side of a stake, one about an inch above the other. Then stand astride the 2-by-4, brace it by holding a sledge hammer against its inner face, and drive the nails through the stake and into the board. Nail the other stakes to the form board in the same way. Now set 2-by-4 form boards for the other straight, raised edges, following the procedures described in Step 2 and here.

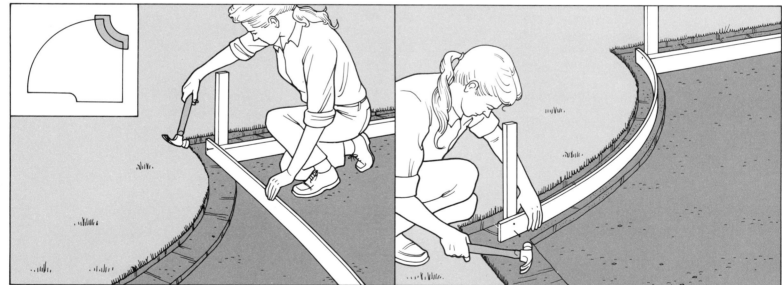

5 **Making a curved form section.** To create a separate curved length of form for raised edging bricks — like the section indicated in the inset — start with a strip of flexible hardboard long enough to complete the curve with several inches to spare. Place the face of one end of the hardboard against the butt end of the 2-by-4 that forms the adjacent straight section. Align the hardboard's top edge with the top edge of the 2-by-4 and drive one finishing nail to hold the strip in place (*above, left*). Now bend the hardboard strip to the desired curve, mark a position behind it for

a stake that will hold it in place, and release the strip. Drive the stake and bend the hardboard, letting the strip follow the gradient of the earth (here, the curved section slopes down toward the mowing edge). Fix the hardboard to the stakes with finishing nails (*above, right*), then drive another finishing nail through the strip into the end of the 2-by-4 where the curve began. Finally, saw off the extra hardboard at the other end of the curve, making the end of the strip flush with the side of the stake.

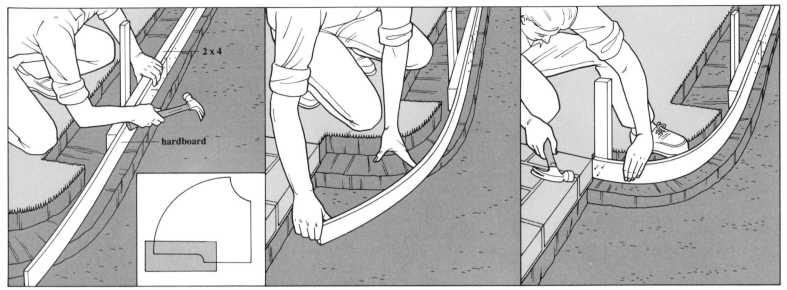

4 **Extending the form around a curve.** Use flexible hardboard to extend the form around a curve from a straight section *(inset, above)*. To provide a continuous flush surface to set the bricks against, the hardboard must run along the whole face of the 2-by-4 as well as forming the curve. If a single strip is not long enough, use two butted end to end, as here. Align their top edges with the top of the 2-by-4 and fix them in place with finishing nails driven through the hardboard and into the 2-by-4 *(above, left)*; set the nails in pairs, one above the other, at intervals of about 10 inches. Next, bend the loose end of the hardboard to the de-

sired curve *(above, center)*, mark a spot on the ground just behind the end of the curve by scratching the earth with the claw part of your hammer, and release the hardboard. Drive a stake into the earth at the marked position. Then bend the hardboard again; holding its end against the stake with one hand and bracing the middle of the curved portion with your foot *(above, right)*, nail the hardboard to the stake with finishing nails. Drive additional stakes behind the hardboard if necessary to maintain the curve, and nail the hardboard to them in the same way.

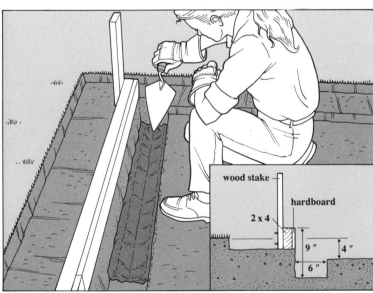

6 **Preparing a trench for vertical bricks.** Along all the inner faces of the form sections that you have constructed for raised edging bricks, dig a trench about 6 inches wide that reaches 9 inches down from the top edges of the 2-by-4s and hardboard *(inset)*. Mix about half a bucketful of mortar. Starting at the end of a straight section of the form, use a mason's pointed trowel to spread a layer of mortar a little more than 1 inch thick along the bottom of a 2-foot stretch of the trench; do not spread the mortar over too long a section, or it might dry before you set bricks in it. With the trowel's pointed tip, make a groove in the mortar 2 inches from the form and parallel to it *(above)*. The furrow will provide room for the mortar to spread out when bricks are pressed into it.

7 **Laying vertical edging bricks.** Set a brick on end into the mortar with one narrow edge butted against the form. Press down on the brick until its top is about ¼ inch above the top of the form. Then tap the top of the brick with the butt of the trowel handle until the brick's top is flush with the top of the form. Now set another brick into the mortar hard against the first. When you have laid bricks along the whole stretch of mortar, pile extra mortar against the bottom of their exposed edges to hold them firmly against the hardboard or 2-by-4. Proceed by spreading another stretch of mortar and setting more bricks. Lay the vertical bricks for all the raised edgings the same way, fanning bricks to fit the curved sections of the form *(above)*. ▶

8 **Marking the height for surface bricks.** Let the mortar dry for one and a half hours. Then, at each end of each straight row of vertical edging bricks, measure 1½ inches down from the top of the end brick and draw a chalk mark there. Tie a chalk line around one of the end bricks at the 1½-inch mark, stretch it taut, and tie it against the 1½-inch mark at the other end. At the center of the row, snap the chalk line crisply to leave a chalked line 1½ inches from the top of the whole row *(above)*. For the curved sections of raised edging, measure and mark each brick individually, 1½ inches from the top.

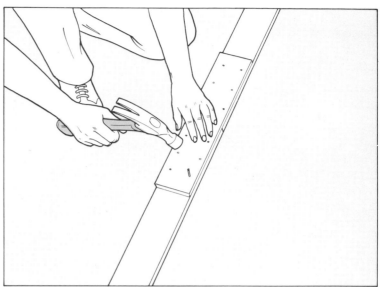

9 **Splicing two hardboard strips.** Where you need a very long piece of hardboard for a separate, curved section of the form — such as the long mowing edge indicated in the inset in Step 10 — butt the ends of two strips together. Then lay a short strip — roughly 2 feet long — over the seam where the two butted ends meet. On each side of the joint, drive six finishing nails through the short piece into the hardboard underneath.

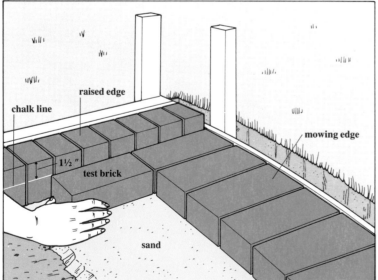

12 **Laying the mowing edge.** Spread a 2-inch-thick, 8-inch-wide layer of mortar along a short section of the curved hardboard. Make two furrows in the mortar parallel to the form. Lay a brick flat in the mortar, with one end butting against the form. Tap the brick with the trowel handle until its upper face is flush with the hardboard's top edge. Lay the other edging bricks the same way, as close together as possible. Then pile some sand against the bricks' exposed ends. With a board or a rectangular trowel, tamp the sand, making it level with the bottom of the edging bricks. Check the depth of the sand bed by putting a brick on it next to the edging bricks *(above)*. Its top should align with the tops of the edging bricks.

13 **Preparing the sand bed.** Spray the earth inside the terrace edges with a hose until the water thoroughly dampens the ground but is not puddling. Holding the handle of a tamper firmly with both hands and standing with your feet apart, tamp the ground until the whole area is compacted. Next, shovel coarse sand onto the tamped earth until the terrace site is covered with sand slightly more than 2 inches deep — just a little higher than the sand against the edging bricks. Now tamp the sand *(above)* until the sand bed is compressed and level; work backward from one end of the terrace to the other so you do not walk on sand you have already tamped.

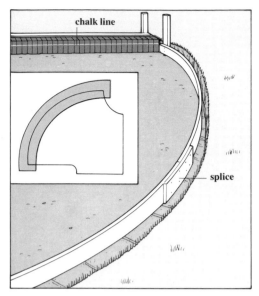

chalk line

splice

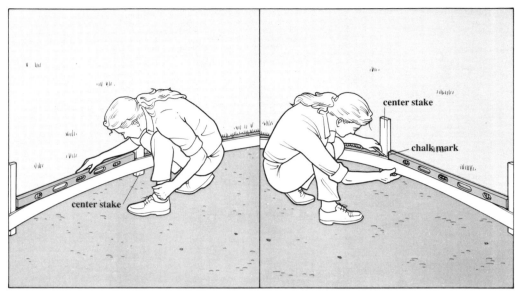

center stake

center stake

chalk mark

10 **Preparing for a mowing edge.** Dig the shelf along a proposed mowing edge (*inset*) down to the 4-inch depth of the general excavation. Bend the spliced-together pieces of hardboard to fit the curve (making sure the 2-foot splice is on the outside of the curve) and drive stakes behind each end. Align the top edge of each end of the hardboard with the chalked line on the vertical edging bricks, and nail the strip to the stakes.

11 **Adjusting the pitch of the curve.** Drive additional stakes behind the hardboard, one of them at the center of the curve. Rest a long carpenter's level — if possible, at least 48 inches long — on top of the hardboard strip to one side of the center stake (*above, left*). Note the bubble reading on the level. Then place the level on the strip to the other side of the stake. The bubble reading should be identical to the first one. If not, raise or lower the center of the curved strip until the two readings are the same. Then mark the position of the hardboard on the stake (*above, right*), remove the level and nail the hardboard to the stake at the marked position.

14 **Preparing screed guides.** Wrap one end of a long string around a spare brick and place the brick just outside the curved mowing edge. Pull the string taut across the edging bricks to the opposite side of the terrace and tie it to a second spare brick. Lay this brick flat in the sand next to the raised edging bricks, making sure that its upper surface — and the string — is level with the chalked line on the vertical bricks. Set another brick under the midpoint of the taut string. This brick's upper face should touch the string without pushing it up; if the brick is too high or too low, adjust the amount of sand underneath it and tamp the sand around the brick to this level. The bottom surfaces of this brick, the brick against the raised edge and the bricks of the mowing edge will provide a guide as you screed, or level, the sand (*Step 15*). ▶

15 **Screeding the sand bed.** Use a straight 2-by-4 that is long enough to reach from just inside the edging bricks to the leveled sand around the brick under the string's midpoint. Rest one end of the board's narrow edge on the leveled sand against the edging bricks and the other end on the leveled sand around the midpoint brick. Applying even pressure with both hands, draw the 2-by-4 screed across the sand toward your knees *(above)*. Go back over the same area, tamping the sand firmly with the 2-by-4. Then screed the section again. Level the entire sand bed in this manner, removing the midpoint brick while you can still reach it. Then remove the excess sand scraped up by the screed.

16 **Laying down roofing felt.** With scissors or a utility knife, cut as many 4-foot-long sheets from a roll of roofing felt as you need to cover the sand bed. To avoid disturbing the leveled sand with your knees and feet, kneel on a scrap of plywood; have a second scrap within reach so you can move from one section to the next without displacing any sand. Starting at one end of the terrace, lay the sheets of roofing felt on the sand, butting — not overlapping — their edges. Cover the entire sand bed with roofing felt.

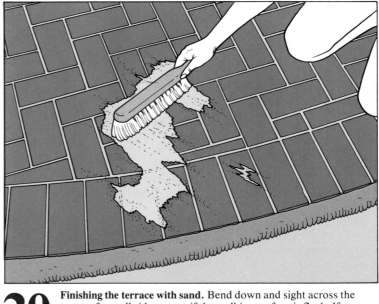

19 **Mortaring edging bricks.** After all the bricks have been set in place, remove the edging form: First extract the duplex nails with a claw hammer and pull up the 2-by-4s and their stakes; then work up the stakes and hardboard of the curved sections. Mix some fresh mortar and pile a 1½-inch-thick layer of it along the outside of the edging bricks. When the mortar has dried, cover it and fill the rest of the trench with mulch or dirt.

20 **Finishing the terrace with sand.** Bend down and sight across the terrace from all sides to see if the walking surface is flush. If any bricks are too high, tap them down lightly with a rubber mallet. If a brick is too low, pick it up and add some sand underneath it. When the surface is flush, throw a ½-inch layer of fine silica sand over the bricks. Using a brush or a broom, sweep the sand into the joints between the bricks *(above)* until the joints are filled completely with sand. Then spray the terrace with water to compact the sand. Sweep a second, thinner layer of sand over the brick surface into the joints to complete the terrace.

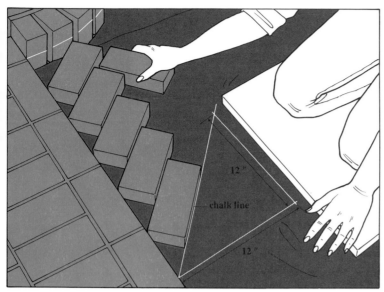

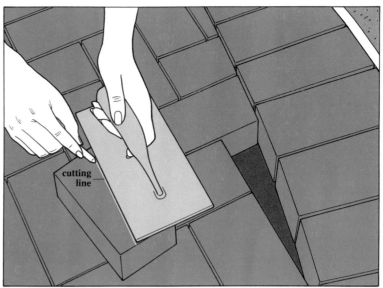

17 **Laying the surface.** Here, the herringbone pattern begins with whole bricks at the house steps; but to cut as few bricks as possible, start along the longest straight edge. At one end use a carpenter's square to chalk on the roofing felt a line 12 inches long, perpendicular to the edge. At the far end of that line, draw another 12-inch line perpendicular to the first. Then connect the ends of the lines with a diagonal line. Lay a brick along the diagonal, setting one corner against the edging row. Complete the row with parallel bricks as close together as possible. Then set the bricks of the next row into the Vs formed by the first row, as shown above. Use a carpenter's level to make sure all the bricks are at the same height.

18 **Measuring for cut bricks.** After you have covered as much of the terrace area as possible with whole bricks, measure an unfilled space that requires a partial brick and mark a brick accordingly. First use chalk and a straightedge or, as here, a rectangular trowel to draw the cutting line across the face of the brick. With the aid of a carpenter's square, extend the line down the sides or ends of the brick, perpendicular to the face. Then turn the brick over and mark the bottom face with a chalk line connecting the lines on the sides or ends. Cut the brick along the lines, following the instructions in the box below, and set it in its space. Measure for, cut and lay the rest of the required partial bricks the same way.

Cutting Bricks

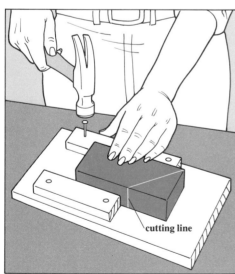

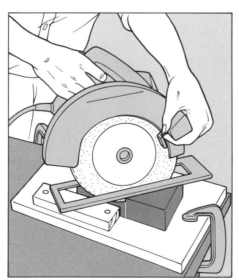

1 **Making a jig.** Set a marked brick on a piece of plywood. Nail a strip of scrap wood onto the plywood against one lengthwise edge of the brick. Push a second scrap strip against the brick's opposite side; the brick should fit tightly in the space between the strips. Nail the second strip in place.

2 **Scoring the brick.** Clamp the jig to a work surface. Set a circular saw with a carbide masonry blade for a ¼-inch cut. Wear goggles to protect your eyes from flying brick fragments and dust. Then slowly guide the saw blade along the brick's marked cutting line, making a ¼-inch-deep groove in the brick. Remove the brick from the jig.

3 **Splitting the brick.** Place the brick, scored side down, in some sand. Set the blade of a brickset — a wide masonry chisel — upright on the cutting line, with the blade's beveled edge facing the waste part of the brick. Using a 4-pound sledge hammer, split the brick by striking the handle of the brickset squarely with a quick, forceful blow.

A Diversity of Designs with Bricks

Their uniform rectangular shape and relatively small size make bricks easy to arrange in many designs suited for sand-based patios. Probably the easiest design to install is the running bond *(below, left)*. The bricks are simply set in straight rows, staggered so that the middle of each brick lines up with the ends of the bricks in adjacent rows.

The basket-weave pattern *(below, center)* and the diagonal herringbone pattern shown in the terrace on the preceding pages give a more dramatic-looking effect. And both are locking patterns: Each brick is held in place by bricks that are perpendicular to it. Such tight locking stabilizes these designs so bricks are less prone to move out of position with weather and wear.

A ladder-weave pattern *(below, right)* sets rows of horizontal bricks between rows of vertical bricks. The vertical rows then act almost like arrows to direct a viewer's eye.

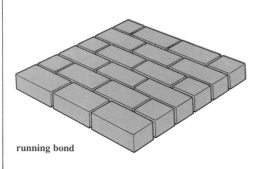

running bond

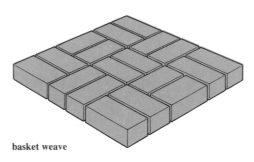

basket weave

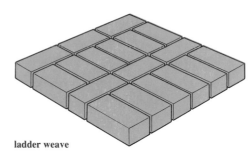

ladder weave

A Sampler of Pavers

Like bricks, precast concrete pavers such as those shown below can lend a variety of effects to sand-based patios and walkways. These pavers are 2 to 2½ inches thick and range in size from 12-inch rounds to rectangles 12 inches wide by 18 inches long.

Small stones embedded in the molded concrete give so-called exposed aggregate pavers *(below, left and second from left)* a skid-resistant texture that blends especially well with rustic surroundings. The rectangular pavers fit into patios or walks; the round ones can become steppingstones.

Colored pavers are made with concrete that is tinted so the color goes all the way through. Their smooth surface makes them appropriate in formal gardens. Rectangular styles are easiest to install, but interlocking styles that fit together like pieces of a jigsaw puzzle *(below, fourth from left)* will prove more resistant to shifting and heaving as weather changes.

Finally, concrete rounds that simulate cross sections of a tree trunk *(below, right)* produce country-style steppingstones that are impervious to wood rot and insect damage.

exposed aggregate block   **exposed aggregate round**   **tinted block**   **tinted interlocking units**   **concrete tree round**

Laying a walk of flagstones and bricks

Flagstones are among the handsomest and most natural of paving materials for a garden path, as illustrated below. Here, square-cut slabs of bluestone counterpoint the red brick rectangles that frame them.

Flagstones are cut from many different types of rock. Common bluestones and sandstones, which range in color from pink to dark blue, can be trimmed to smaller sizes with a brickset and a sledge hammer. Slates, usually purple or grayish in color, are harder, more durable and more difficult to cut. Flagstones vary in thickness from ½ to 3 inches. Select stones of roughly equal thickness so that the paved surface will be level. Have the stones delivered close to your building site, and use a dolly to move them.

Because flagstones are large slabs—18-inch squares are best for mortarless walks — the paving project will proceed quickly. However, the stones require a stable foundation to prevent them from shifting with the weather; you will need to provide a thick, solid subbase.

The techniques for laying flagstone are similar to those for setting bricks *(pages 52-59)*. The area to be paved must first be staked, then graded and excavated; or you may decide after grading to lay the foundation and flagstones on top of the earth, building up the surrounding land.

The foundation's first layer is a 4-inch subbase, made of a dry mortar mix. Tamp and level the mortar with a screed.

Then make a setting bed by spreading a layer of stone dust — finely crushed gravel that compacts well and resists shifting. (If stone dust is not available in your area, use sand instead). For a plain flagstone pavement, the setting bed should be 3 inches deep. If you are combining different materials, prepare a shallow setting bed first and lay the thicker, accent material in place. Then add more stone dust to build up the setting bed so the flagstones will lie flush with the accent material. Tamp and level the bed.

Finally, lay all the flagstones in the desired positions. If any stone wobbles, pry it up with a crowbar and add more stone dust where needed. If a stone is set too high, gently tap it down with a rubber mallet. When all the flagstones are in place, brush stone dust into the crevices until they are completely filled. Spray the flagstone walkway with water to compact the stone dust; fill the crevices with more stone dust if necessary.

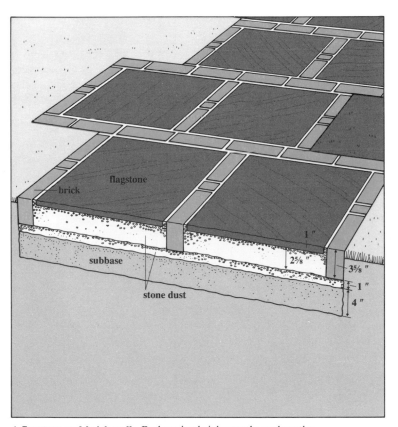

A flagstone-and-brick walk. Red paving bricks neatly enclose the Pennsylvania bluestones in the staggered design of this garden path. A 4-inch subbase of sand and dry cement is covered by a 1-inch layer of stone dust. Whole and cut bricks are then set on edge to form rectangular frames for the stones, and the spaces inside these frames are filled with 2⅝ inches of stone dust. Slabs of 1-inch-thick flagstone are lowered into the frames on top of the stone dust. Finally, the joints between stones and bricks are filled with more stone dust to smooth the surface.

Building a parquet-patterned deck

Elements of house and yard blend in this deck's combination of the formal pattern of a parquet floor with the rough simplicity of unfinished wood. The deck planks are supported by a specially designed frame of angled beams and joists *(opposite)*; other patterns can be laid on simpler underpinnings *(pages 74-75)*. No matter what the

design, a deck is relatively simple to assemble, requiring only basic carpentry tools and techniques.

Start by mapping the area on graph paper *(pages 52-53)*, then make a scale drawing of the deck. The one shown here is designed to fit into an L-shaped space where it can be anchored to two intersecting house walls; it must also be a square

for the decking planks to fit correctly.

The holes for supporting posts should be at least 24 inches deep; in many areas they must be deeper, to reach below the frost line. Local building authorities can specify the necessary depth of footings and tell you about building-code requirements that apply to railings and stairs. The deck shown here, because it is very

low, needs no stairs or railing; most codes require them for decks that are higher than 2 feet above the ground, but you might decide to add them for safety and convenience in any case.

If you are required to have a building permit before starting construction, you will probably have to submit a drawing with your application; even if that is not required, it is wise to have an engineer or building inspector review your plans.

This deck is connected to a frame house with wood siding. Special techniques are needed to remove aluminum siding or to attach ledgers (the framing timbers that you must bolt to the house) to a masonry foundation. You may also have to remove an existing step to allow you to attach the ledger below the door; if you are faced with such a situation, consult a builder to decide on your best course of action. You may want to hire a subcontractor for some stages of the job, such as removing siding, digging postholes or pouring concrete. Otherwise, enlist enough helpers for the heavy work.

To extend the life of the deck, use weather-resistant wood such as cedar, redwood or pressure-treated pine. If you economize, use pressure-treated wood at least for the posts and beams, which are most subject to moisture-induced rot.

Estimate the amount of lumber you will need by counting the number of boards of each size in your scale drawing. Find out whether your lumber supplier will accept returns of uncut lumber; if so, you can order extra joist and decking planks to avoid delays caused by underestimating your needs or measuring incorrectly. Have the supplier unload the lumber and bagged concrete close to the building site, but out of the way of traffic.

Most of the work is done with common carpentry tools such as a claw hammer, line level, combination square, pry bar, power drill, handsaw, chisel and circular saw. Heavy-duty power saws and drills speed the cutting and drilling of large, pressure-treated timbers; these tools are available at tool-rental centers. You will also need a shovel, hoe, posthole digger and wheelbarrow for digging postholes and mixing and pouring concrete.

Working with heavy materials is tiring work; for safety's sake, allow plenty of time for each stage of the job and stop when you begin to tire. Working with care can also help prevent wasted time and materials; following the old carpenter's adage ''Measure twice, cut once'' is a particularly good idea when the lumber in question is a valuable 18-foot 2-by-10.

Materials List

All lumber is No. 2-grade pressure-treated yellow pine.

2 x 10	2	2 x 10s, 18 ' long, for long diagonal beams
	4	2 x 10s, 14 ' long, for outer beams and ledgers
	4	2 x 10s, 8 ' long, for short diagonal beams
2 x 8	2	2 x 8s, 14 ' long, for fascias
	8	2 x 8s, 10 ' long, for joists
2 x 6	8	2 x 6s, 14 ' long, for decking
	8	2 x 6s, 12 ' long, for decking
	10	2 x 6s, 10 ' long, for decking
	10	2 x 6s, 8 ' long, for decking
4 x 4	2	4 x 4s, 10 ' long, for posts
	1	4 x 4, 8 ' long, for post
Hardware	24	2 x 6 single joist hangers, with nails
	20	½ " hex-head lag screws, 3 " long
	6	½ " hex-head lag screws, 4 " long
	10	½ " carriage bolts, 8 " long
	8 lbs.	eightpenny galvanized-steel common nails
	5 lbs.	sixteenpenny galvanized-steel common nails
Concrete	4	bags ready-to-mix concrete, 80 lbs. each

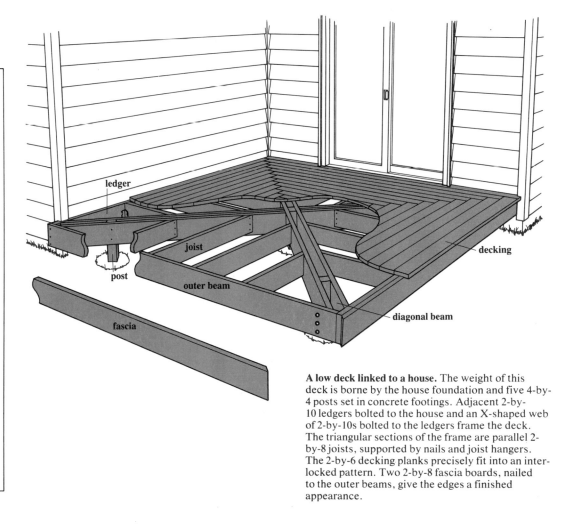

A low deck linked to a house. The weight of this deck is borne by the house foundation and five 4-by-4 posts set in concrete footings. Adjacent 2-by-10 ledgers bolted to the house and an X-shaped web of 2-by-10s bolted to the ledgers frame the deck. The triangular sections of the frame are parallel 2-by-8 joists, supported by nails and joist hangers. The 2-by-6 decking planks precisely fit into an interlocked pattern. Two 2-by-8 fascia boards, nailed to the outer beams, give the edges a finished appearance.

1 Marking the side of the house. Mark a point 1½ inches below the center of the door-sill of the house. Drive a small nail at the mark, leaving about an inch protruding, then tie a string to the nail. Stretch the string taut to the outside corner of the house. Attach a line level at the center of the string, then adjust the string until it is level, and make a pencil mark where it meets the outside corner of the house.

Repeat this procedure on the other side of the nail to mark the inside corner of the house, then remove the nail and drive another at the mark at the inside corner. Stretch a chalk line between the marks at each corner and snap it *(left)*.

Then mark a level line on the adjacent side of the house, beginning at the nail in the inside corner.

4 Nailing the outer beams. Cut two 2-by-10 outer beams, one 3 inches shorter than the width of the deck, the other 1½ inches shorter. Position one end of the long beam with its broad face against the end of the long ledger and its top flush with the top of the ledger. While your helper holds the beam roughly level, drive three sixteenpenny nails through the beam into the end of the ledger *(left)*. Prop the beam's free end on scrap lumber. Attach the other beam to the other ledger similarly, then connect the two beams at the outer corner by driving three sixteenpenny nails through the long beam into the end of the short beam.

2 **Cutting through wood siding.** Set the blade of a circular saw to a cutting depth of ¼ inch, then align the blade with the chalked line at an outside corner of the house. Starting at the outside corner, saw a groove in the siding along the chalk-marked cutting line, until the base plate of the saw hits the inside corner of the house. To continue the groove into the corner, position a broad wood chisel on the chalked line and drive it into the siding with a hammer; repeat this action until you reach the corner. Slip a pry bar under the bottom of the siding and pry the siding outward until it breaks cleanly along the groove, exposing the wood sheathing or framing underneath. Use the same technique to remove the siding on the adjacent side of the house.

3 **Installing ledgers.** Cut two 2-by-10 ledgers, one 3 inches shorter than the planned deck width, the other 4½ inches shorter. Fit the long ledger below the door, with its top edge against the bottom of the cut siding and one end butted into the inside corner; nail its ends to the exposed wood of the house with sixteenpenny nails. Position the short ledger against the adjacent wall and nail it in place. Mark a center line along the length of each ledger. Starting from the inside corner, mark 16-inch intervals on the center lines of each ledger. Using a ⅜-inch twist bit, drill 3-inch-deep pilot holes through each mark into the framing timbers behind the ledgers. Drive ½-by-3-inch hex-head lag screws into each pilot hole, using a socket wrench or a box wrench to tighten them firmly.

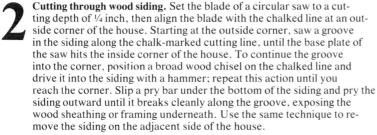

5 **Leveling the frame.** Set a carpenter's level on top of one of the outer beams near its intersection with the other beam. Remove the props from beneath the frame and have your helper adjust the height of the frame until the bubble of the level is centered. Hold a scrap board against the outside of the beam about 2 feet from the beam's end, with one end of the scrap resting on the ground, and nail the scrap to the beam with two eightpenny nails. Check the level again to ensure the frame is still level, then nail a second scrap board to the adjacent beam in a similar manner. ▶

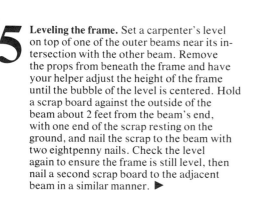

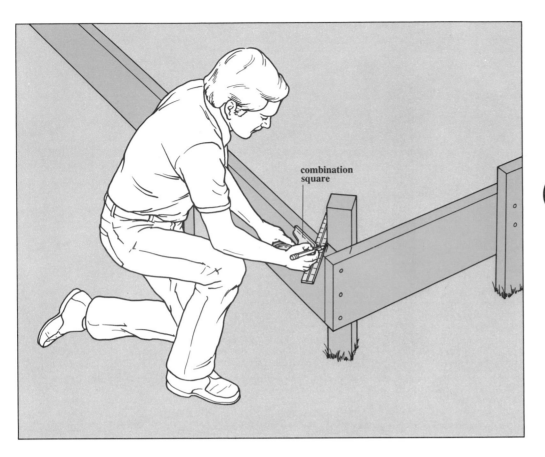

combination
square

6 **Measuring for beams.** Stand a piece of 4-by-4 in the outside corner of the frame, with two corners touching the intersecting beams. Use a combination square to align the face of the post at a 45° angle to the beams, then make a mark at the edge of the top of each beam where the post corner touches it. Mark the beams and ledgers at the three other corners of the frame similarly.

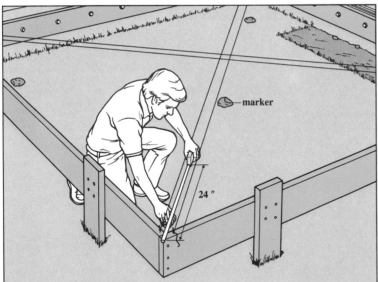

marker

24 "

8 **Marking for postholes.** Gather five rocks or brick scraps to serve as markers. Place the first marker directly below the intersection of the four strings at the frame's center. From one corner of the frame, measure 24 inches along the strings toward the center, placing a marker directly beneath the strings at this point. Mark the three other corners similarly.

9 **Digging postholes.** Untie the strings from the nails, leaving the nails in place. Scratch a circle 18 inches in diameter around the rock marker at the outside corner. Remove the marker and use a posthole digger to begin a hole the size of the circle. Place your feet well apart, lift the post-hole digger a couple of feet off the ground, then thrust the blades into the earth. Pull the handles wide apart to lift the dirt out of the hole, then release the dirt in a pile off to one side by pushing the handles together. Make the hole deep enough to extend 24 inches below the frost line, keeping the sides vertical. Dig the four other holes the same way.

7 **Laying out a string outline.** Drive a small nail partway into each of the marks you made in Step 6 at the corners of the frame. Tie a string around one nail and stretch it diagonally across the frame to the corresponding nail at the opposite corner. Then stretch a second string parallel to the first, between the other two nails at those corners. Stretch strings in the same way between the nails at the other two opposing corners so that the four strings intersect to make a small square at the middle of the frame.

10 **Measuring for beams.** With a 25-foot steel tape, measure the distance from one of the nails at the intersection of the beams to the corresponding nail at the opposite corner. Then make a pencil mark 1 inch from the end of an 18-foot 2-by-10, and from this mark measure along the length of the board the same distance as the nail-to-nail measurement you just made. Mark that place. Now draw lines across the board's broad face, perpendicular to its edge, at the marks.

Set the blade of your circular saw for a 45° beveled cut *(page 45, Step 18)*. Set the 2-by-10 across two sawhorses and make beveled cuts at each of the lines, in each case positioning yourself so the saw blade is angled toward the center of the board. Measure and cut the second 2-by-10 beam to the same length. ▶

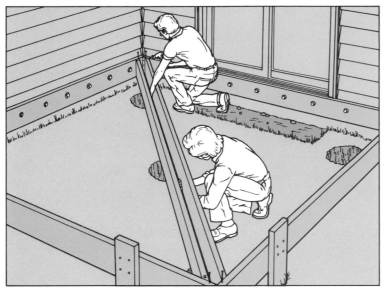

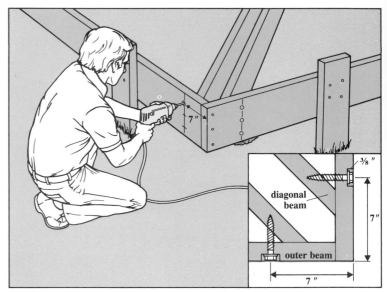

11 **Nailing diagonal beams.** Carry a diagonal beam inside the frame; have your helper hold up one end while you position the point of the other end at the inside corner under the marker nail in the ledger perpendicular to the door. Align the top of the beam with the top of the frame and drive three sixteenpenny nails at an angle through the broad face of the beam into the ledger. Nail the other end of the beam to the outer corner with one angled sixteenpenny nail.

Secure each end of a second diagonal beam parallel to the first with sixteenpenny nails driven at an angle through the top edge of the beam into the frame. At the inside corner, drive another nail through the beam's bottom edge into the frame.

12 **Securing the beams.** Starting from the outer corner, measure 7 inches along one of the framing beams and draw a pencil line down the outside face of the beam. Draw cross marks on this line at the center and 2 inches from the top and bottom. Use a power drill with a ¾-inch spade bit to bore a hole ⅜ inch deep at each cross mark; then switch to a ⅜-inch spade bit and bore a hole 4 inches deep at the center of each large hole, drilling through the framing beam into the diagonal beam. Use a socket wrench to drive a ½-by-4-inch lag screw through each hole into the diagonal beam *(inset)*. Drill and screw the outer end of the other diagonal beam in the same manner.

14 **Hanging the short beams.** Use the steel tape to determine the distance between the back of one joist hanger and the corresponding marker nail in the corner facing the joist hanger. Mark this distance from one end of a 2-by-10, then make a 45° beveled cut at the mark, cutting with the blade angled inward under the measured section of the 2-by-10 *(Step 10)*. Set the square end of the short beam into the joist hanger, pushed against the long diagonal beam, and nail the beveled end to the frame at the corner as shown in Step 11. Drive nails into the short beam through the predrilled holes in the hanger. Cut and hang the three other short beams to complete the X-shaped framework.

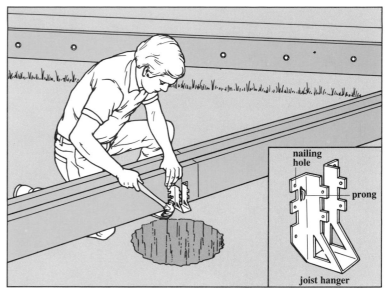

13 **Measuring for short beams.** Stretch strings between the marker nails in the empty corners as shown in Step 7. Mark the points where the strings cross the diagonal beams, then align the ruler of a combination square with each mark in succession and draw lines down the outer faces of the beams from the marks *(above).* Remove the strings. Position a metal joist hanger *(inset, above right)* with its right inside edge aligned with the left-hand pencil line on one beam. Align the bottom of the joist hanger with the bottom of the beam and tap the prongs of the hanger into the beam. Drive nails provided by the hanger manufacturer through the predrilled holes *(above).* Position another hanger similarly, with its left inside edge aligned with the other pencil line on the beam, and nail it in place. Nail joist hangers to the other diagonal beam similarly.

15 **Setting the posts.** Shovel 4 inches of gravel into the central posthole, then measure the distance from the gravel to the tops of the beams above it. Cut a 4-by-4 post about 6 to 8 inches longer than this measurement and slip the post between the beams, resting its bottom on the gravel. Place a carpenter's level against one side of the post and adjust the post until it is plumb, then hold the post as you drive two eightpenny nails through one beam into the post. Use a handsaw to trim the top of the post flush with the tops of the beams.

Now drill two ½-inch holes through the beam, the post and the opposite beam, 2 inches from the top and bottom of the beam. Put a ½-by-8-inch carriage bolt through each hole, slip a washer over the end and turn a nut onto the bolt, tightening it with a wrench. Use the same procedure to position and secure posts in the four other holes. ▶

16 **Pouring concrete footings.** Empty the contents of a bag of ready-to-mix concrete into a wheelbarrow placed just outside the deck framework. Add water to the concrete mix according to the manufacturer's directions and mix the concrete with a hoe. Use a shovel to transfer concrete into a posthole until the level of the concrete is slightly above the surface. Shape the concrete into a shallow conical mound around the base of the post. Shovel concrete into the remaining holes and shape it in the same way. Allow the concrete to set according to directions on the bag before removing the temporary supports from the outer frame.

chalk line

24 "

18 **Marking the beams.** Drive small nails partway into each heavy pencil line on the ledgers. Attach the hooked end of a chalk line to a nail and stretch the chalk line across the frame to the corresponding pencil mark on the opposite outer beam. As your helper holds the chalk line in place on the pencil line, snap the string to leave chalked lines across the diagonal beams. Repeat this procedure for each marker nail on the two ledgers, stretching the chalk line to the opposing outer beams and marking the diagonal beams. Then remove the marker nails.

17 **Marking joist locations.** Lightly mark on the top of one outer beam the midpoint of that side of the frame, measured from corner to corner. Draw a heavy pencil line 12 inches from each side of this point. From each of these heavy lines, measure toward the frame's corners, making additional heavy lines at 24-inch intervals. Repeat this procedure on the other outer beam and the two ledgers.

midpoint

19 **Marking the joist positions.** Find a bevel-ended 2-by-10 scrap and create a marking jig by drawing a pencil line along the center of both narrow edges. Position the beveled edge of the jig against the face of a diagonal beam, aligning the jig's center line with a chalked line on the top of the beam. Then mark a line on top of the beam at each side of the jig.

Use a combination square to draw a vertical line down the face of the beam from each mark. Use the jig and square to make identical lines at each chalked line on the diagonal beams. Similarly mark the outer beams and ledgers, using the square end of the jig centered under the pencil lines drawn in Step 17.

center line

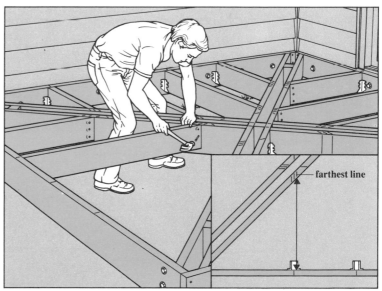

20 **Hanging the joists.** Fit a scrap of 2-by-8 into a joist hanger, then position the hanger so its inside edges are aligned with a pair of lines on one outer beam and the top of the scrap is flush with the top of the beam. Secure the hanger *(Step 13)*. Place joist hangers at the other marked points on the outer beams and ledgers. Then measure from the back of a joist hanger to the farthest line of the corresponding pair on the facing diagonal beam *(inset)*. Cut a 2-by-8 joist to this length, with one end square and the other end beveled *(Step 10)*. Nail the square end into the joist hanger and the beveled end to the beam as shown in Step 11. Repeat this procedure to cut and hang the remaining joists ▶

farthest line

21 **Attaching fascias.** Measure one outer side of the deck frame, from corner to corner. Add 1½ inches to your measurement, then use this dimension to mark and cut a 2-by-8 fascia with one end beveled to a 45° angle, as shown in Step 10. Align the top of the fascia with the top of the outer beam and the obtuse angle of its beveled end with the outer corner. Using sixteenpenny nails, secure the fascia in place at each end and at 16-inch intervals in between, setting one row of nails an inch from the top and another an inch from the bottom. Cut another fascia 1½ inches longer than the other outer side of the frame, and nail it in place with its beveled end butted against the bevel of the first fascia.

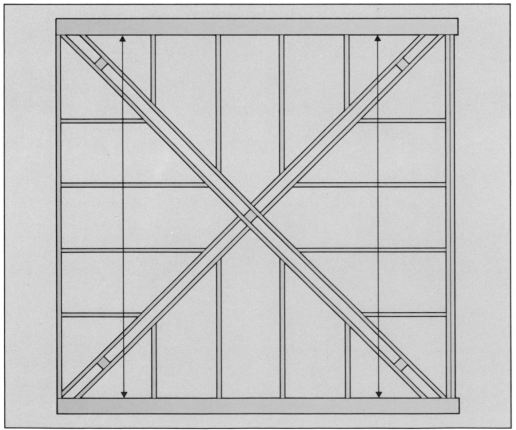

23 **Positioning the second deck plank.** Cut a 2-by-6 1½ inches longer than the side of the deck opposite the first plank. Lay it on the frame along that side, allowing 1½ inches of the long edge to overhang the fascia. Measure the distance between the two planks at one end. While your helper holds this end in place, measure the distance between the planks at the other end; adjust the loose board until this measurement is the same as the first, so the boards are parallel. Nail the second plank to the beam and joists as shown in Step 22.

22 **Laying the first deck plank.** Measure one inner side of the completed frame, from the inside corner to the outside of the fascia. Cut a 2-by-6 plank 1½ inches longer than this measurement. Lay the plank on the ledger and joists, butted into the inside corner and against the side of the house.

To make a notch for the vertical house trim, mark the edge of the plank where it touches the trim at the outside corner. Remove the plank and use a handsaw to cut 1 inch into the narrow face at this mark. Use a broad chisel to break off the corner of the plank up to the saw cut. Replace the plank and nail it to the frame with eightpenny nails driven into the ledger every 16 inches; drive additional nails into each joist 1 inch from the plank's outer edge.

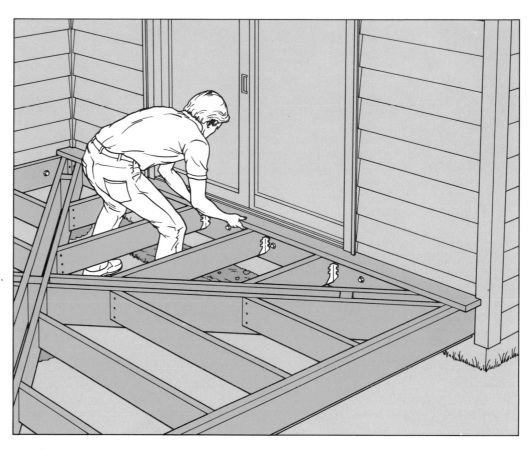

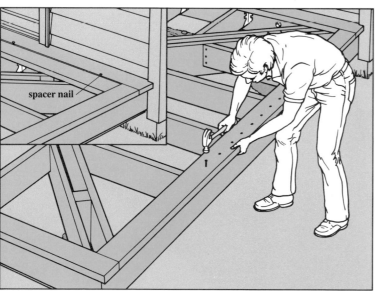

24 **Adding more planks.** Cut two planks ¼ inch shorter than the distance between the first two. Position one against the house, with an equal gap at each end. Notch the plank where it abuts the corner (Step 22), and nail it down. Lay the other plank over the opposite outer beam so it overlaps the fascia by 1½ inches; nail it parallel with the opposite plank. Tap sixteenpenny nails partway into the top edge of joists near the ends and center of each installed plank (inset) to help maintain a constant space between adjacent planks. Cut and fit the remaining planks in pairs, each pair perpendicular to the last one. Push each plank against the spacer nails and nail it in place, then move the spacers.

25 **Fitting the final decking.** As you near the center of the frame with the decking planks, begin measuring the remaining gap before you cut planks to fill it. When the width of the opening is 17 inches or less, use one of the patterns shown above for the final pieces. If the gap is less than 11½ inches wide (left), cut two pieces of decking to length, then rip-cut (page 123) each to a width ¼ inch less than half the opening, and nail the planks in place. If the opening is more than 11½ inches wide (right), cut three planks to the length of the opening; rip-cut each piece to a width ¼ inch less than one third of the opening, and nail them in place with equal spacing between them.

Patterns and Supports

The pattern of planks for the surface of a deck dictates the design of the substructure, which must support each decking plank at both ends and at intervals along its length. The frames supporting the three decking patterns shown here are variations of a design that is simple to build; more complicated patterns, like the one on page 62, usually require more complicated underpinnings. Other factors also affect the frame's design. The size of lumber used and the spacing of posts, joists and beams are interrelated; specific requirements are governed by building codes, which vary by locality.

The deck plans shown here are based on a layered frame: Beneath the decking are the joists, supported at the house end by joist hangers nailed to a ledger. Near their outside ends the joists are toenailed to the top of a split girder, made of paired 2-by-10s bolted to opposite sides of posts set in concrete. Between the joists, timber bridges keep the joists from tilting.

The techniques for building these decks are similar to those shown on pages 63-73. Ledgers are bolted to the house, then postholes are dug below the frost line and posts set in concrete. A line is drawn on each post at the level of the bottom of the ledger, and the posts are cut at the lines. The girder timbers are then bolted in place flush with the tops of the posts; the joists are secured to the ledger with joist hangers and toenailed to the girder. Bridging pieces cut from joist timbers are nailed between the joists. Finally, the decking is nailed to the joists in the desired pattern.

Although these plans for 12-by-12-foot decks will meet the requirements of most local building codes, check your own plan with local authorities before building, to make sure the deck is both safe and legal.

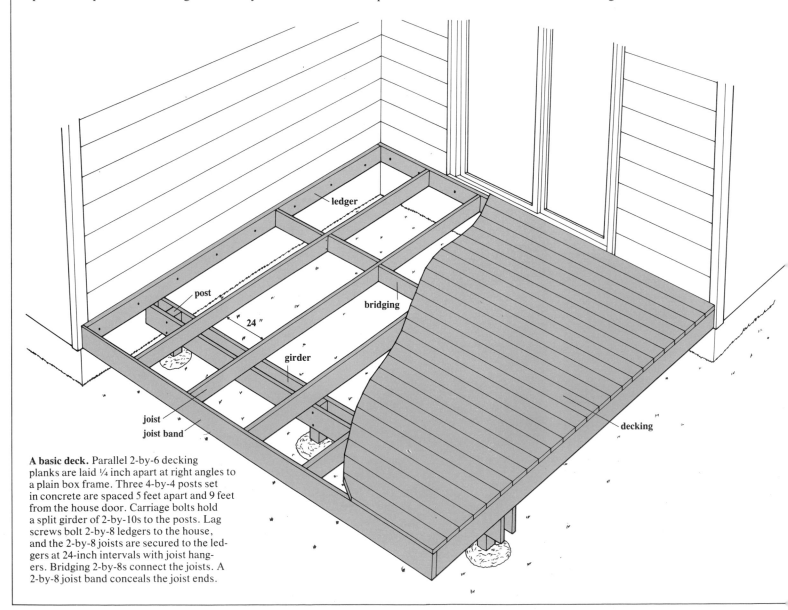

A basic deck. Parallel 2-by-6 decking planks are laid ¼ inch apart at right angles to a plain box frame. Three 4-by-4 posts set in concrete are spaced 5 feet apart and 9 feet from the house door. Carriage bolts hold a split girder of 2-by-10s to the posts. Lag screws bolt 2-by-8 ledgers to the house, and the 2-by-8 joists are secured to the ledgers at 24-inch intervals with joist hangers. Bridging 2-by-8s connect the joists. A 2-by-8 joist band conceals the joist ends.

ledger

post

24″

bridging

girder

joist

joist band

decking

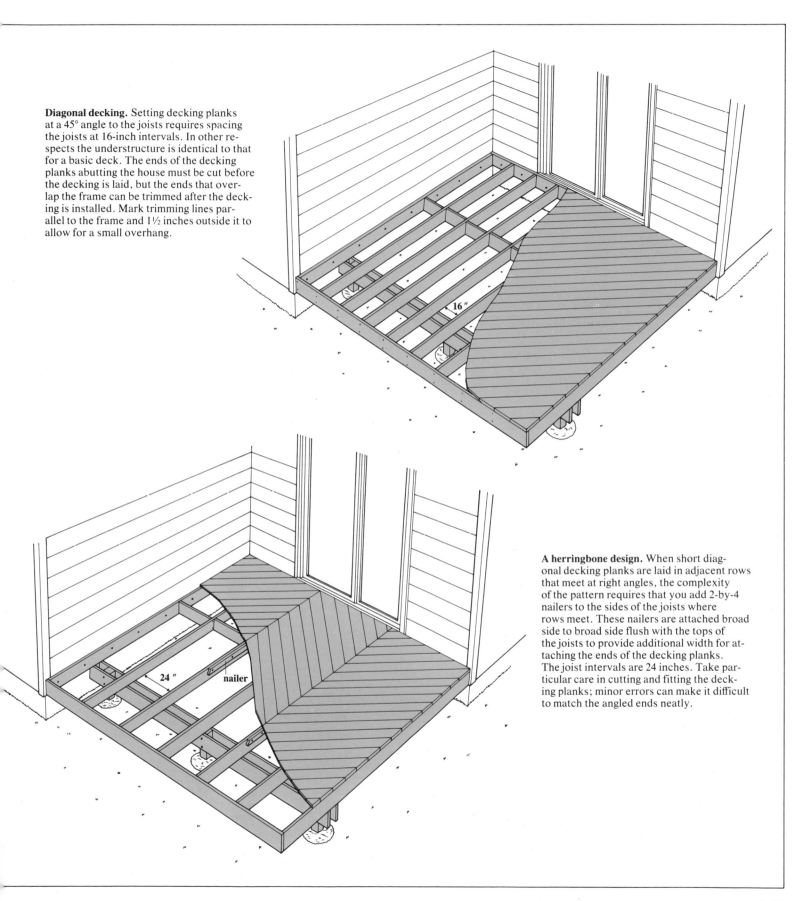

Diagonal decking. Setting decking planks at a 45° angle to the joists requires spacing the joists at 16-inch intervals. In other respects the understructure is identical to that for a basic deck. The ends of the decking planks abutting the house must be cut before the decking is laid, but the ends that overlap the frame can be trimmed after the decking is installed. Mark trimming lines parallel to the frame and 1½ inches outside it to allow for a small overhang.

16 "

24 "   nailer

A herringbone design. When short diagonal decking planks are laid in adjacent rows that meet at right angles, the complexity of the pattern requires that you add 2-by-4 nailers to the sides of the joists where rows meet. These nailers are attached broad side to broad side flush with the tops of the joists to provide additional width for attaching the ends of the decking planks. The joist intervals are 24 inches. Take particular care in cutting and fitting the decking planks; minor errors can make it difficult to match the angled ends neatly.

Fountains and pools

Adding a pool magnifies the attractions of a garden by reflecting flowers, foliage and the changing sky overhead. And a fountain will contribute other pleasures — the sound of moving water, patterns of ripples, the sparkling play of light.

With a minimum of disruption, you can bring water to your garden by building a shallow pond aboveground *(pages 80-87);* a larger pond, capable of supporting plants and fish, must be belowground *(pages 88-91).* Either type requires a totally waterproof lining. Preformed liners of glass-reinforced plastic offer one answer, but they come only in small sizes and a limited number of shapes. Greater variety is possible with flexible plastic sheeting, which molds itself to the shape of the hole you put it in.

Whether you are building a new pond or refurbishing an old one, you should also plan to install a submersible electric pump that will draw the water continuously through a filter *(pages 78-79).* You can then maintain a tranquil pool by pumping the clean water back in below the surface, or you can make the pump provide a spray of water through a fountain.

As the photographs on these two pages demonstrate, you can achieve any of a wide range of effects by your choice of fountain head — the part that protrudes above the pool's surface and shapes the spray of water. Be sure to select a fountain head that will match its site: A showy vertical spray that looks good in a large, formal pool is out of place in a small pond nestled among mossy rocks. Consider the biology of the pool as well: Fish benefit from the turbulence of a lively fountain, but water plants are better served by the gentler circulation provided by a spray ring *(below)* or a bubbler *(bottom right).*

water inlet

Fountain heads to shape the spray. The pattern of spray at left is created by water spurting from the nozzles of a plastic ring *(left).* The legs of the ring are cut to size so the nozzles barely protrude above the surface of the pool. Water from a pump enters through an inlet in the bottom of the ring. The various spray patterns at right are created by interchangeable fountain heads *(insets)* screwed to a stand that doubles as a water conduit. Vertical sprays *(top row)* protrude just above the surface and create turbulence in the pond, as does the dome fountain *(bottom left),* which stands high enough to create a hemisphere of falling water. The water-lily bubbler *(bottom right),* set a few inches above the surface, provides gentler water circulation.

Keeping water in motion

For lasting beauty, a pool must be kept clean — a tall order out of doors. Dust and other wind-blown detritus are constant problems; so too is algae, which can quickly cover the surface and sides of a pool. The answer lies in an efficient circulation and filtration system, readily available from suppliers of garden equipment. For a large pond, you will probably need a system with separate units *(below);* for a smaller pond, you may be able to use a system that combines pump and filter in one compact apparatus *(box, lower right).*

Plan your system around the pump, which must be large enough to recirculate all of the water every two hours. To determine the volume of your pool in gallons, first multiply its surface area (in square feet) by its average depth (in feet); multiply the result by 7.5. A pump's capacity, or flow rate, is measured in gallons per hour. To be effective, its flow rate should equal half of the pool's volume. The filter you choose should match the flow rate of the pump.

If you want a fountain, try to match the flow rate of your fountain head to the capacity of your pump or get a water restrictor *(far right)* to regulate the flow. And get enough hose so you can position the water intake as far from the fountain head as practical, to promote maximum circulation. Ready-made fountain stands are available, but you can easily fit pieces of steel pipe together to create a stand *(near right)* that can support a variety of fountain heads.

When the circulation system is in place and the pool is filled, only the fountain head and the pump's electric cord will be above the surface. Plug the pump into an outlet that is well away from the pool and equipped with a ground-fault interrupter. This special sort of circuit breaker shuts off power to the pump the instant that any current leaks into the water. Be sure to use only heavy-duty extension cords specifically rated for outdoor use.

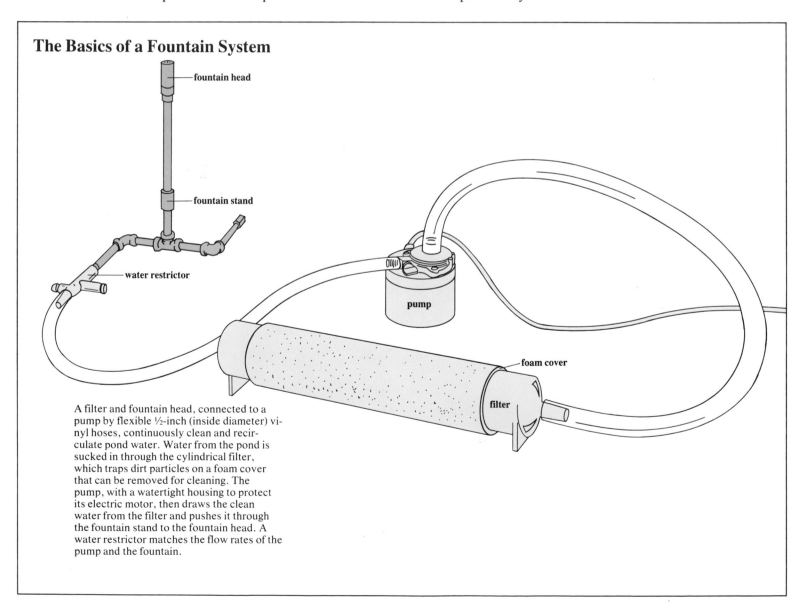

The Basics of a Fountain System

fountain head

fountain stand

water restrictor

pump

foam cover

filter

A filter and fountain head, connected to a pump by flexible ½-inch (inside diameter) vinyl hoses, continuously clean and recirculate pond water. Water from the pond is sucked in through the cylindrical filter, which traps dirt particles on a foam cover that can be removed for cleaning. The pump, with a watertight housing to protect its electric motor, then draws the clean water from the filter and pushes it through the fountain stand to the fountain head. A water restrictor matches the flow rates of the pump and the fountain.

A Homemade Fountain Stand

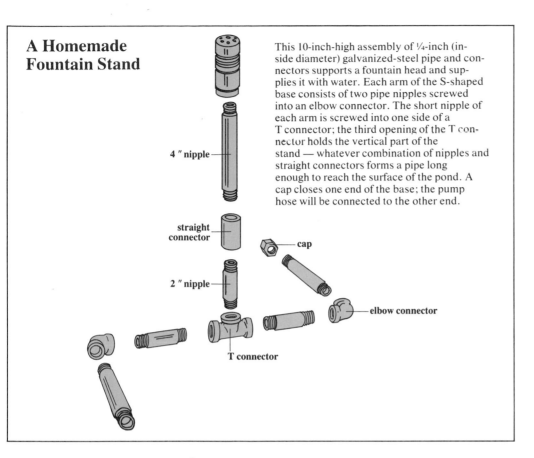

4 " nipple

straight connector

cap

2 " nipple

elbow connector

T connector

This 10-inch-high assembly of ¼-inch (inside diameter) galvanized-steel pipe and connectors supports a fountain head and supplies it with water. Each arm of the S-shaped base consists of two pipe nipples screwed into an elbow connector. The short nipple of each arm is screwed into one side of a T connector; the third opening of the T connector holds the vertical part of the stand — whatever combination of nipples and straight connectors forms a pipe long enough to reach the surface of the pond. A cap closes one end of the base; the pump hose will be connected to the other end.

Regulating Water Flow

To keep a pond properly filtered, the pump and fountain head should handle the water at the same rate — ideally recirculating it on a two-hour cycle. If your fountain head has a smaller capacity than your pump, add a water-restrictor valve, such as the one shown below, between the pump and the fountain. The adapter's small end fits into the valve; the large end is threaded inside to hold the pipe. With the valve attached, you can govern the flow of water with the control knob; excess water will go directly to the pool through the shunt.

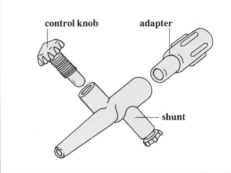

control knob   adapter

shunt

A Compact Circulation System

This circulation system for small ponds puts the pump inside a plastic filter box, thus eliminating the need for a hose between these two components. The pump draws pond water into the box through a foam filter, then pushes clean water out through a flexible plastic hose that may be connected to a fountain. The foam filter is sandwiched between a stationary slotted support and a removable outer grill that allows access to the filter for periodic cleaning.

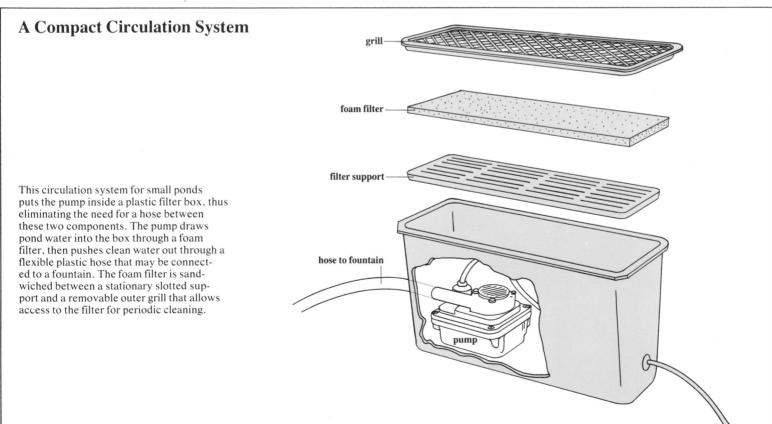

grill

foam filter

filter support

hose to fountain

pump

A brick pool above the ground

Nothing makes a garden more inviting than an ornamental pool with a trickling fountain, and few pools are as easy to create as the one shown below. Because this pool sits on, not in, the ground, little digging is required — just enough to clear the site and, if necessary, make it level. Although the pool is built of bricks, no mortar is needed; the water is held in by a double lining of polyethylene plastic.

The pool requires a level site that is 7 feet from front to back and 7½ feet wide. To conceal the pump's power cord and water hose, which emerge from the structure's back, position the pool against a wall or fence. And place it within reach of an electrical outlet that has a ground-fault interrupter (*page 78*).

When ordering the 500 bricks needed for the project, ask for standard-sized wire-cut paving bricks (*page 53*). Clear a delivery space close to the site; if the space is on your lawn, protect the grass with boards laid across 2-by-4s. Also se-

lect a place to put the 4½ cubic feet — about 500 pounds — of builder's sand you will need. If you have trouble getting that small an amount delivered, you can buy the sand in bags and transport it yourself.

Polyethylene is available where fountains and water-gardening supplies are sold, at building-supply stores, nurseries and some brickyards. The plastic sheeting must be 6 mils (6/1,000 of an inch) thick and 12 feet wide (it is folded to a much narrower width before it is rolled). You may have to buy a roll 100 feet long, even though the pool requires only a sixth that much. Save the leftover polyethylene, because after a couple of years your pool liner may develop leaks; since no mortar is involved, it is easy to remove the upper layers of brick and reline the pool. Use black polyethylene; any color would look unnatural, and black will give your pool an illusion of depth.

The fountain seen here consists of a fluted, hand-crafted ceramic bowl and a hook-shaped flexible copper tube that

spills water into the bowl. But you can use any fountain that returns water to the pool (*pages 76-77*).

You will also need some wood. Four 5-foot 2-by-4s will be nailed together to make a form, the framework that serves as a guide for laying the bricks. An 8-foot 2-by-4 will be used as a straightedge in laying out the pool, and other 2-by-4s will be used to smooth the sand. Make sure that the 2-by-4s are straight. Any piece of plywood about 3 feet square will serve as a board to kneel on so you can work without disturbing the leveled sand.

Before you begin to build, paint the pump, its power cord and the water hose with black interior/exterior spray enamel to make them less visible in the pool. If your fountain is like this one, bend the flexible copper tubing and spray it with enamel in a color to match the bowl.

This pool is not deep enough for fish or water plants. But you can landscape it by surrounding it with shrubs, ground cover and potted plants and flowers.

Materials List

Bricks	500 standard-sized wire-cut paving bricks
Plastic liner	1 roll 6-mil-thick black polyethylene, 12 ' wide
Sand	4½ cubic feet (about 500 lbs.) builder's sand
Pump	1 submersible pump, with a rated capacity of 200 gallons per hour
Water hose	½ " (inside diameter) vinyl hose, 10 ' long
Copper tubing	½ " (outside diameter) flexible copper tubing, 6 " long
Finishing materials	1 can interior/exterior spray enamel in a color to match fountain's bowl (for copper tubing) 1 can black interior/exterior spray enamel

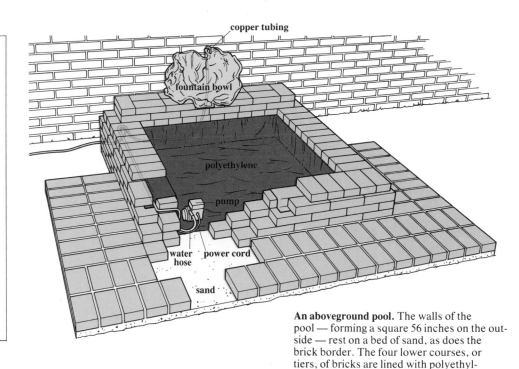

An aboveground pool. The walls of the pool — forming a square 56 inches on the outside — rest on a bed of sand, as does the brick border. The four lower courses, or tiers, of bricks are lined with polyethylene held in place by the bricks above them. The pump is submerged in a front corner of the pool; its power cord and water hose run between the side wall's inner and outer bricks to the back of the structure. From there the hose goes to the fountain, the cord to an electrical outlet.

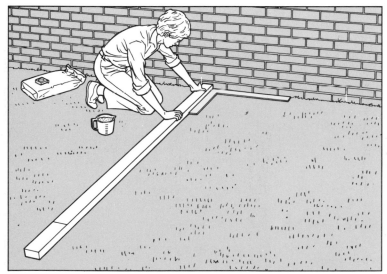

1 **Clearing the site.** On the wall, make a chalk mark where you intend to center the pool's back. Measure 45 inches to each side of that point, and mark those places on the wall. Place the end of a straight 8-foot 2-by-4 against the wall, with the outer edge of the board's broad side against the left-hand mark on the wall. Use a carpenter's square to make sure the 2-by-4 is perpendicular to the wall *(above)*. Measure 84 inches from the wall along the 2-by-4, and mark the board there. Now fill a plastic measuring cup with sand and sprinkle the contents along the 2-by-4's outer edge, stopping at the 84-inch mark. Make another 84-inch line of sand perpendicular to the wall from the right-hand mark; then connect the front ends of the two lines with a third line, forming a rectangle 84 inches deep and 90 inches wide. Clear this area of grass, plants and stones with a flat-edged shovel, and use a short-toothed rake to level the soil.

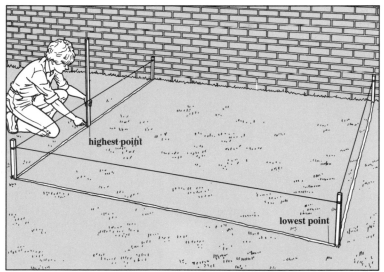

2 **Leveling the ground.** Make four wood stakes about 12 inches long. Mark each with a pencil line 1 inch from its top, and hammer two stakes into the ground at adjacent corners of the rectangle. Lay the 8-foot 2-by-4 on edge across their tops and place a carpenter's level on it to see which stake is higher; drive the higher stake down until both stakes are level. Drive in another stake at an adjacent corner and make its top level with the first two. Do the same to the fourth stake. Now run a taut string around the rectangle, tying it to each stake at the pencil mark. Measure from the string to the ground at several points on each side: The largest measurement indicates where the ground is lowest. Use a flat-edged shovel to shave off the higher parts of the perimeter and fill in the lower parts, frequently measuring from the string to the ground; then bring the interior to approximately the same level, checking by eye. ▶

3 **Building a form.** Measure 56½ inches from right to left along a broad side of each of four 5-foot 2-by-4s and make a mark there. (This measurement represents the length needed for seven 8-inch-long bricks laid end to end, allowing ½ inch for variations in brick size.) Use a carpenter's square to draw a perpendicular line across each board at the mark. Now draw another, parallel line across each board 1½ inches to the left of the first. Arrange the 2-by-4s to form a square with overlapping corners *(above)*; butt the unmarked end of each board between the double lines marked across the adjacent board. Now drive two twelvepenny nails through the side of each overlapping board into the end of the 2-by-4 that butts against it; do not drive the nails all the way home.

4 **Squaring the form.** At the midpoint you marked on the wall in Step 1, and at points about 2 feet to each side of it, set one arm of the carpenter's square horizontally against the wall and measure 10 inches out from the wall on the other arm. Mark those spots by pushing twelvepenny nails partway into the soil. Now measure for and mark the midpoint of the inner side of the form's back board. Position the form so that the back board's midpoint is aligned with the midpoint on the wall and the back board's inner surface rests against the line of nails. Set the carpenter's square into one rear corner of the form *(above)* and shift the side board, if necessary, to make the 2-by-4s meet in a 90° corner. This will ensure that all the corners are squared. Remove the nails from the soil.

7 **Checking for uniform height.** Using the carpenter's level, check along all four sides of the square for bricks that are out of alignment with their neighbors. If a brick is too high, lift it out of its place, remove a little of the sand from its bed with a trowel, return the brick to its position and use the butt end of the trowel to tap it back into place *(left)*. If a brick is too low, put a little more sand underneath it.

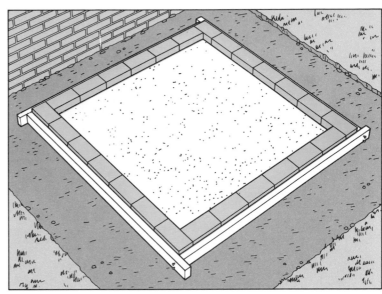

5 **Making a level bed of sand.** Shovel enough sand onto the area inside the form to make a bed about 2 inches deep. Kneeling on a piece of plywood about 3 feet square so your knees do not disturb the sand, use the narrow side of a 4-foot-long 2-by-4 to tamp down a section of the bed, then drag the 2-by-4 over the tamped-down area to level it — a technique known as screeding. Repeat this process over the entire sand bed. At 1-foot intervals from back to front and from side to side, lay a carpenter's level on top of the 2-by-4 and check to see that the surface is level *(above)*, adding or removing sand with a trowel as necessary to produce a uniformly level site.

6 **Laying the outer perimeter of the first course of bricks.** Lay a row of end-to-end bricks — stretchers, in bricklayers' terminology — against each wall of the form as shown above: seven bricks each along the two sides and six bricks each across the back and the front, with the ends of those last two rows butting against the side rows. If there is a gap at the end of any row, move the bricks in that row slightly apart to divide the space evenly among them.

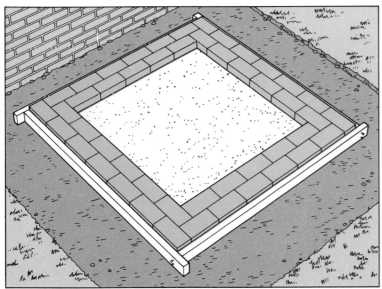

8 **Laying the first course's inner perimeter.** Lay the inner perimeter of the first course of bricks as shown above: six stretchers along each side and five across the front and the back. Then hold the carpenter's level across the double rows to see if the inner bricks are level with the outer ones. Correct any height discrepancies by removing or adding sand *(Step 7)* under the bricks in the inner perimeter.

9 **Adding other courses of bricks.** Build the outer perimeter of the second course of bricks as shown above; this time the ends of the side rows butt against the front and back rows, so that each brick spans the joint of the two bricks below it. Then fill in the inner perimeter of the second course of bricks as seen here. Now remove the form, taking care not to disturb the alignment of the bricks, and pile a little extra sand against the outside of the walls to hold in the sand under the bricks. Next, build the third course of bricks, duplicating the pattern of the first course *(Steps 6 and 8)*. For the fourth course, lay only the inner perimeter, following the pattern of the inner perimeter of the second course *(above)*. ▶

10 **Cutting the polyethylene.** Measure 100 inches along both sides of the folded, 12-foot-wide polyethylene and make a small cut with scissors at each point. Lay a 2-by-4 across the plastic at the cuts and score along it with a scissors blade *(above)*. Cut the plastic along the scored line. Then unfold the strip to get one thickness. Measure 100 inches along the 144-inch sides, and cut small notches. Fold the plastic in half lengthwise so the notches meet; measure 100 inches along the fold, and cut a notch there. Score a line between those notches and cut along it to create a 100-inch square. Now cut another square the same size, and staple one square atop the other at a few places along the edges.

11 **Installing the polyethylene.** Spread the polyethylene over the structure so that roughly the same amount overlaps each of the four walls. Push the plastic down onto the sand and set the piece of plywood in the center of the pool. Kneeling on the plywood, smooth the polyethylene into each corner. Then stand outside the pool to smooth the liner against and over the pool's walls *(above)*.

14 **Trimming the polyethylene.** Beginning at the front left-hand corner, set aside the outer corner brick and use scissors to cut away the excess polyethylene there; trim the plastic down to a 1½-inch-wide margin on top of the third-course outer bricks below. Now remove the second brick, cut away the excess plastic underneath it, then put the first brick back in place and remove the third brick *(left)*. Work your way around all four sides in this way, until the edge of the polyethylene is completely trimmed and hidden beneath the outer bricks of the fourth course.

12 **Installing the pump.** Slip the vinyl water hose an inch onto the pump's discharge nozzle. Set the pump in a front corner of the pool — on the side nearest the electrical outlet. Pull apart the top corner bricks nearest the pump, making a gap of about ½ inch, and push the polyethylene down into the space. Wedge the water hose and the cord into the gap, with the water hose on top. (If the gap is too small, fold back the polyethylene from the side wall and push each brick in the top row toward the back of the pool to make room.) Now run the hose and cord along the outside of the polyethylene-covered row of bricks to the back, as seen above.

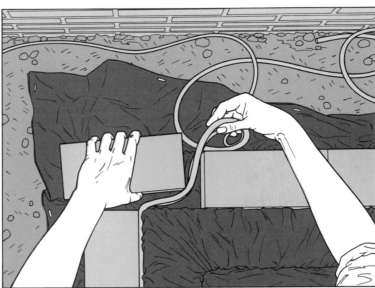

13 **Hiding the cord and hose with bricks.** Duplicating the pattern of the second course of bricks *(Step 9)*, start laying the outer perimeter of the fourth course along the side where the hose and cord are located. If the hose and cord take up so much space that the outer bricks hang over the edge of the wall below, push the bricks of the inner perimeter inward so that they slightly overhang the inside of the wall instead. After laying the whole outer perimeter of the fourth course, wedge the hose and cord between the two outer bricks at the back of the pool that are nearest to the corner *(above)*.

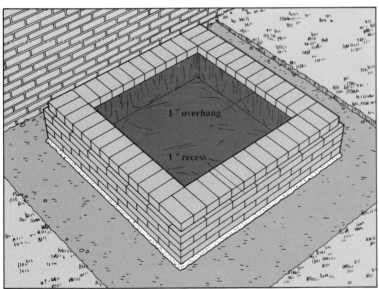

15 **Laying the fifth course of bricks.** Beginning at the left-hand corner of the front wall, place a brick with its short side facing forward — in what bricklayers call the header position — then push this brick 1 inch back from the front of the wall and 1 inch in from the side. Lay a row of headers recessed in this way across the front of the pool *(above)*; the outer side of the last header should be recessed 1 inch from the edge of the wall below. Then lay rows of headers along the side walls as shown, their outside ends recessed 1 inch from the edges of the bricks underneath, and fill in across the back wall with another row of recessed headers. All the headers will overhang the inner edges of the walls below by 1 inch.

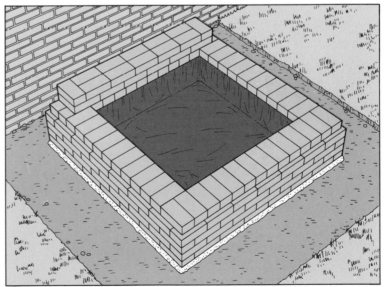

16 **Building up the back wall.** At the back left-hand inside corner, lay a lengthwise brick — a stretcher — recessed half a brick length from the edge of the side wall. Lay five more stretchers from left to right across the back of the pool; then lay a second line of six stretchers immediately behind this row. Returning to the left-hand side of the pool, lay one header on top of, and flush with the outside edges of, the bricks below. Then lay five stretchers and another header. Behind the five stretchers lay five more stretchers, so the two courses appear as above. ▶

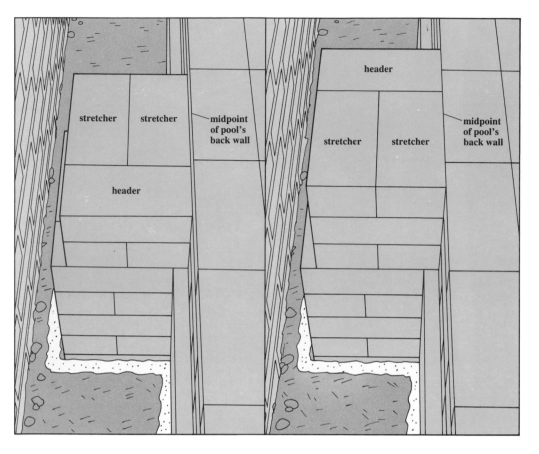

17 **Building a fountain support.** Set a header and two stretchers on the ground against the pool's back wall, arranging them like the three bricks atop the stack at far left; align the midpoint of the bricks' combined length with the midpoint of the wall.

Dribble lines of sand around the bricks to mark their position, then set them aside. Use a trowel to dig a hole inside the sand lines about 3 inches deep. Put enough sand into the hole so that when the bricks are moved back into position, their top surfaces will be level with the bottom of the bricks in the wall's lowest course.

Place the bricks on the sand, and on top of them arrange two stretchers and a header like the three bricks atop the stack at near left. Alternating the pattern with each course, build a stack of bricks eight courses high. When you reach the level where the wall's bricks are recessed 1 inch, butt the bricks of the fountain support structure against the recessed wall bricks, as seen here.

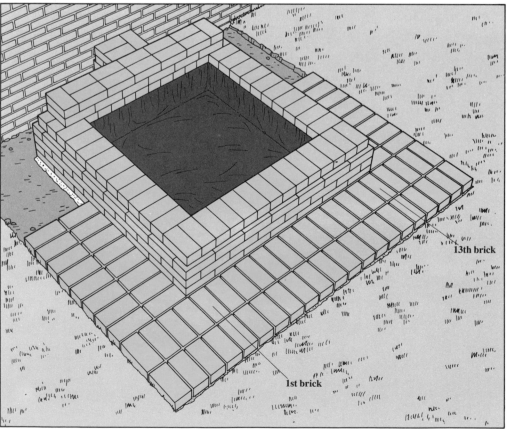

20 **Laying the border.** Beginning at the pool's front left-hand outer corner, lay a header about ¼ inch to the right of the corner and the same distance from the pool's front wall. Lay 12 more headers from left to right along the front of the pool, spacing them just a little more than ¼ inch apart. The 13th brick should be roughly ¼ inch to the left of the pool's right-hand front corner; if it is not, adjust the spaces between the bricks. Lay four more headers at each end of the row, to the edges of the sand bed.

Then lay a second row of 21 headers about ¼ inch in front of the first row. Next, fill in each side border with two eight-brick rows as seen at left, again leaving roughly ¼ inch between bricks. When all the bricks are laid, make any spacing adjustments necessary to obtain straight outside edges for the border.

Now spread a thin layer of sand over the border and use a broom to sweep the sand into the joints between bricks. Pack soil around the border's outside edges to cover the sides of the bricks.

18 **Marking the limits of the border.** Measure 34 inches along the side of the pool from the front corner, and mark the side wall there with chalk. Align the outside edge of one arm of a carpenter's square with that mark while butting the square's other arm against the pool's wall. Sprinkle sand along the outside edge of the first arm (*above*), to make a line across the cleared earth perpendicular to the wall. Follow the same process to make another perpendicular line at the same place on the other side of the pool.

19 **Preparing a sand bed for the border.** Cover the border area — the cleared earth in front of the pool and back along both sides to the sand lines you made in Step 18 — with sand 2 inches deep. Tamp and screed the sand with a straight 16-inch-long 2-by-4 (*above*) and use the carpenter's level to make sure the border is level (*Step 5*).

21 **Installing the fountain.** On top of the back wall and the fountain support structure, position two bricks to create a wide V shape that opens toward the pool. Prop the bowl against the two bricks; if necessary, wedge chips of hardwood mulch under the bowl to make it stable.

Now insert the straight end of the hooked copper tubing about 1 inch into the end of the water hose. Hang the tubing's hooked end over the top of the bowl (*right*). Run water into the pool from a garden hose until the water is just below the top edge of the plastic. Make sure the pump is completely submerged; then plug in the pump.

A water garden with a plastic liner

ater gardening — the art of cultivating aquatic plants in a pond or pool — is nearly as old as civilization itself, yet only recently, with the advent of tough plastic sheeting made from polyvinyl chloride, or PVC, has it become a pastime almost anyone can enjoy. A garden pond like the one shown below consists of an excavation lined with PVC and bordered by masonry to hold the sheet in place. Such a pond can easily be built in any of a variety of shapes and sizes at a fraction of the cost and time required for a cement pool — and it will last for years.

The flexible plastic liner that makes this method of construction possible consists of a single sheet of 20-mil-thick PVC.

When the pond is filled, the plastic liner readily conforms to the contours of the excavation, forming a watertight seal against the bottom and sides. Flagstone paving makes a perfect border to secure the edges of the PVC where they overlap the rim of the pond and protect the plastic from the weakening effects of the sun's ultraviolet rays.

PVC is sold by pool and garden suppliers in a wide range of sizes. When you order a plastic liner, always specify fish-grade PVC: Some types of plastic sheeting are treated with chemicals that can be harmful to plants or fish. Flagstone paving is readily available from building-supply firms or quarries in either 12-inch-wide rectangles or irregularly shaped slabs.

The key to any successful garden pond is planning. The best site is one with plenty of direct sunlight. Water lilies will need at least five hours of sunshine a day in order to blossom luxuriantly. Even if you are not growing lilies, avoid shaded areas under or near large trees, where falling leaves, twigs, petals or fruit may pollute the water and kill any fish you stock.

Pick a spot within reach of a hose so you can easily fill the pond. A nearby electric outlet is also a convenience if you plan to install a fountain or a water-recirculating pump.

How large you make your pond depends on the size of your yard and its proportions. Large ponds are generally more satisfying than small ones, both esthetically and in terms of aquaculture: The smaller the pond, the more precarious the ecological balance within the water garden. Try visualizing different-sized ponds in your yard by outlining their dimensions on the ground with a length of hose or clothesline *(Step 1)*. In order to hold an adequate volume of water, no pond should have a surface area smaller than about 40 square feet, or a depth less than approximately 15 inches.

After determining your pond's location and dimensions, calculate the size of the liner required simply by adding twice the depth of the pond to its length and to its width, plus 2 feet more in each dimension to allow for the overlap on all sides. Then follow the step-by-step instructions on these pages to complete the construction.

1 **Orienting the site.** Use a hose or clothes-line to outline the pond in your yard; drive short stakes into the ground at each of the four corners and connect them with string. Check the right angles with a carpenter's square, and adjust the sides until the diagonal lines connecting opposite corners are equal in length. Then mark the outline on the ground with a chalk squeeze bottle, available from hardware stores. Drive a second set of stakes into the ground to represent the outer corners of the 12-inch-wide flagstone paving; connect the outer set of stakes with string, and mark the ground beneath it with a second chalk line.

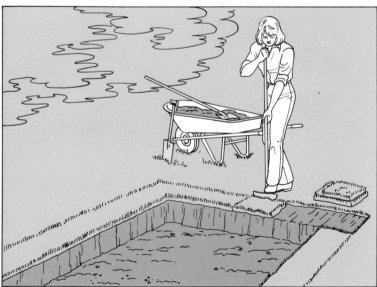

2 **Beginning the excavation.** Remove the stakes from the site and dig out a 9-inch-deep hole inside the pond borders, using a transplanting spade to cut the vertical walls and a shovel to scoop up the loose soil; carry the soil away in a wheelbarrow. With an edge cutter, cut the turf between the pond walls and the border of the flagstone paving into manageable blocks approximately 1 foot square and 1½ inches thick. Lift them out with the transplanting spade or shovel; if you like, you can replant the turf in another section of your yard or garden.

3 **Leveling the banks.** Lay a 2-by-4 on edge across the width of the excavation so its two ends rest on opposite banks of the pond. Place a carpenter's level on top of the board and check the bubble inside the indicator to determine if the banks are level. Proceed to level the banks by removing soil from the higher side with the transplanting spade until the bubble is centered in the indicator. Repeat the leveling process at two or three more points along the length of the hole. Then set a longer 2-by-4 board lengthwise across the excavation and use the same technique to level these banks. ▶

4 **Completing the excavation.** Using the spade and shovel, deepen the hole to 18 inches on three sides of the pond. As you proceed, check the depth of the hole with a 2-by-4 scrap that you have marked at 9 and 18 inches from one end with crayon or heavy pencil. Leave an earthen shelf approximately 9 inches wide along the fourth side of the pond (*left*) to hold marginal plants such as irises and bulrushes, which are grown with their roots covered by only a few inches of water. Use the scrap to check the height of the shelf at two or three points along the bank.

6 **Installing the liner.** Lay the plastic liner loosely over the hole with its edges overlapping the banks on each side; position some of the flagstone paving blocks on the overlap to hold the liner in place. Then slowly fill the pond with water from a hose, allowing the weight of the water to press the liner into the hole and pull the plastic down to match the pond's contours. Move the stones occasionally as the pond fills to let the liner sink in more deeply and to smooth out any wrinkles that develop. Continue filling the pond until the water level rises to approximately ½ inch below the top of the bank.

7 **Trimming the liner.** After the pond is filled, trim the edges of the liner with scissors to leave an overlap of about 10 inches on each side. Reposition the flagstones on top of the overlap, if necessary, to prevent the liner from slipping off the bank as you work.

5 **Layering the floor with sand.** Inspect the bottom and sides of the hole, and remove any sharp stones, tree roots or underground debris that might puncture the plastic liner when the pond is filled with water. Pour a layer of sand approximately 2 inches deep in the bottom of the hole. It will serve as a protective cushion for the liner. Use the back of a tined rake or a stiff push broom to spread the sand into an even layer.

8 **Laying a flagstone border.** Pour a layer of sand 1½ inches deep on top of the PVC over-lap, completely covering the 12-inch-wide border area. Try not to spill any sand into the water. Use a scrap piece of 2-by-4 as a screed to level the sand. Then pave the borders with 12-inch-wide flagstones laid end to end. Pour additional sand on top of the stones and use a stiff broom to sweep it into the gaps between the stones until they are held rigidly in place.

Enlivening enclosures

Fences are, first and foremost, barriers, but they can be so much more. For many city dwellers a fence defines an extra, out-of-doors living room, a place to relax, have a drink, read a book or casually entertain friends while enjoying the privacy of an intimate space.

Just as the walls of a living room can be enlivened by color or crown molding, so a garden enclosure can be improved by some fresh use or treatment of the fence surrounding it. A subtle shadow painted on a wood plank fence, such as in the photograph below, deceives the eye and makes even dull days seem bright. Similarly, a garden area can be made to appear bigger than it is with the addition of a trellis that plays tricks on the eye *(pages 96-101)*.

And sections of fencing strategically placed can make such unsightly but necessary objects as trash cans and coiled hoses disappear *(pages 108-111)*.

A fence can also serve as a support for a plant shelf *(page 94)*, increasing the flowering area of a garden and bringing new color to an ordinarily dull surface. Or a fence can be used for a game board, like the colorful one shown on page 95. Then, too, it can be esthetically enhanced as in the photograph at right, where a simple semicircle relieves the monotony of too many vertical pickets. And in another eye-pleasing effect, a roll-up awning can function as a kind of flexible fence *(pages 116-121)* that will add privacy to a porch while offering protection from rain or the glare of the sun.

The sun seems always to be shining in this backyard, but only because a shadow has been painted on the fence. All you need to create this effect are a carpenter's chalk line, a roll of masking tape, some outdoor paint and a brush. With a helper, stretch the chalk line from the upper corner of one wall of the fence to the ground, and snap it. Place a strip of tape along the line left by the chalk. Then paint or stain the sections of fence on the shadow side of the tape a slightly darker shade than the rest.

Pattern on a Picket Fence

In the photograph at upper right, a graceful semicircle provides a backdrop for a Japanese stone lantern in a restful garden recess. To achieve a similar effect, use boards as wide as the gaps between your pickets. Insert them into the gaps and fix them temporarily in place by hammering a fourpenny galvanized-steel nail partway through each board and into the bottom stringer. Using a pencil and string tied to a nail hammered into the base of the middle picket, draw a semicircle of the desired radius. Remove the new boards and trim them with a saber saw, following the curve of the pencil line. Put the pieces back in place and nail them to the bottom stringer with sixpenny galvanized-steel nails. Then use the same kind of nails to attach the longer pieces to the middle stringer. Secure the shorter ones to the adjacent pickets with fourpenny galvanized-steel nails angled through the top edge of each new board.

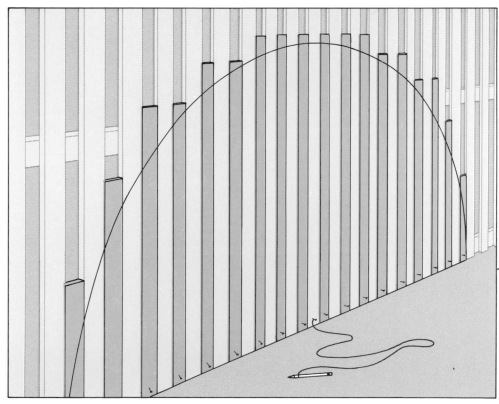

Bringing a Fence to Life with Plants

Lined with pots of flowering impatiens, this simple 2-by-10 shelf of pressure-treated pine puts the garden fence to attractive use. The shelf is supported by the middle fence stringer and by braces positioned every 3 feet. Constructing one like it is a simple task. With the aid of a combination square, draw lines at a 45° angle across a piece of pressure-treated pine 2-by-6 *(below)*; then cut along the lines with a crosscut saw to form braces. Notch each brace so it will fit around the stringer.

With the shelf lying top side up, drill pairs of countersunk screw holes for No. 10 screws 1 foot in from each end and at intervals of 3 feet — one hole 3 inches from the front of the shelf and the other 3 inches from the back. Hammer tenpenny galvanized-steel nails partway into the shelf at 1-foot intervals along the rear, place the shelf on the stringer and finish hammering in the nails. Hold each brace under a pair of predrilled holes and insert an awl through each hole to mark where the screws will go. With a ⅛-inch bit, drill pilot holes through the awl marks. Then attach each brace to the shelf with 2½-inch rust-resistant No. 10 flat-head screws driven through the predrilled holes *(inset, left).* To firmly secure the braces to the fence, hammer fourpenny galvanized-steel nails through each brace into the fence at a point 1¼ inches from the tapered bottom.

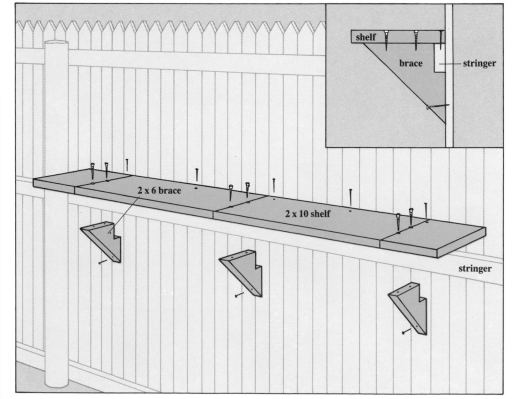

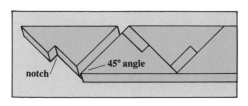

Turning a Fence into a Plaything

Used for a pitch game, this boldly graphic baseball-diamond board can transform a small garden space into a child's playground. To make one, take a piece of ¾-inch exterior-grade plywood 36 inches square and paint it a bright color with glossy or semigloss exterior enamel. Divide the painted board into 12-inch squares and stretch masking tape along the inside edges of the four squares that will remain the background color. Then paint the five other squares a contrasting color. When the paint is dry, remove the tape.

In the meantime, prepare the stencils for applying the graphics. Use the diagram at right. Mark single sheets of stencil paper measuring 12 inches square with 1-inch squares, copy the graphics onto the paper and cut out the designs with a stencil knife. Tape the stencils one at a time to the board and use several light coats of exterior spray enamel of appropriate colors to complete the graphics.

After the paint has dried, drill ¼-inch holes 3 inches in from each of the four corners. Holding the board against the fence, determine the proper height and push an awl through the top hole into the picket to start a channel for a 1½-inch rust-resistant No. 10 round-head wood screw. Drive in the screw. Adjust the board to make sure that it hangs straight, and finish screwing it down.

Intended for small children, this game ignores the rules of baseball. A tennis ball or whiffle ball thrown at the target scores one, two or three points for hitting a number, four for *H* (home run), and nothing for hitting the painted ball or the zeros.

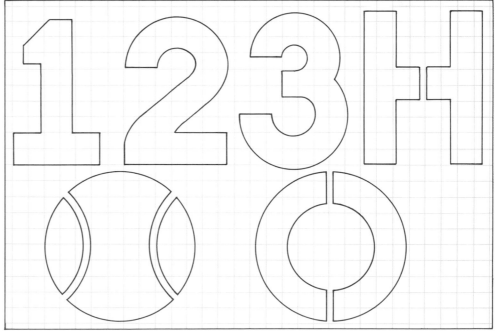

A trellis to create an illusion of space

The fence that confines a yard can also — paradoxically — make the yard seem more expansive when it holds a *trompe l'oeil* trellis such as the one shown at left. *Trompe l'oeil* is French for "trick of the eye," and this trellis's trick, of course, is in appearing to be a passageway that leads through the 7-foot wood fence behind it to a door beyond. A raised path of white gravel and potted arborvitae intensify the illusion.

All this legerdemain is accomplished with simple materials. The trellis is composed of wood lath nailed onto a 3½-by-8-foot panel of exterior-grade plywood; exterior grade indicates that the plies are bonded with waterproof adhesive. For accurate fit, each piece of lath should be sawed to size as you use it, but you can have the plywood cut from a 4-by-8-foot sheet by the lumber dealer. Ask for the ½-foot-wide strip the dealer saws off; its factory-cut edge will serve as an accurate, extra-long straightedge.

Before putting the trellis together, give the fence and the plywood two coats of an identical color of exterior paint; give the lath two coats of a contrasting color. In this case, the fence and plywood are gray, whereas the lath is white. To preserve the plywood, paint both sides and all of the edges. Paint the long edges of the lath; the ends are painted after the lath is nailed in place.

To minimize finicky measurements and bias cuts, the diagonal elements of the design are nailed over one set of framing lath, and then their ends are hidden behind another layer of lath *(pages 98-99)*. Once assembled, the trellis can be mounted on a wood fence merely by nailing it in place. The trellis should be mounted above the soil to keep its base dry year-round.

Materials List

Lumber	1 sheet AD-quality ¾ " exterior-grade plywood, 4 ′ x 8 ′, cut into 1 panel, 3½ ′ x 8 ′ 300 ′ 1⅜ " lath 30 ′ 1⅛ " lath
Hardware	2 oz. ⅞ " galvanized-steel wire brads 12 sixpenny galvanized-steel common nails
Paint	exterior-grade flat latex, white exterior-grade flat latex, gray

The trellis design set out on a grid. All of the lines of the trellis from tower to base, including the walkway and door on which the design focuses, are made of lath. Wide, 1⅜-inch lath is used everywhere but at the door, which is made of 1⅛-inch lath to increase the illusion of distance. To simplify copying the trellis, the design is superimposed on a grid that you can enlarge to any dimensions you like; in the steps that follow, each grid block is treated as a 6-inch square. For further streamlining, the design is bilaterally symmetrical: The left side mirrors the right side.

1 **Drawing the design on the panel.** Set two sawhorses about 4 feet apart to provide a steady base, and put the 3½-by-8-foot plywood panel on them with its smoother side facing upward. Make tick marks denoting the ends of grid lines at 6-inch intervals around all four edges of the panel. Use a piece of chalk and the factory-cut edge of the remaining 8-foot-long strip of plywood as a straightedge to draw the grid lines with chalk. Then, using the scale drawing on page 97 as a guide, transfer the design onto the panel, beginning at the top with the tower design. Draw with a pencil to distinguish the lines of the design from those of the grid; to ensure correct line spacing, lay a piece of lath — either 1⅜ inches wide or 1⅛ inches wide as appropriate — in the position called for by the design, and draw lines on both sides of it *(left)*.

4 **Nailing the lath.** Follow the lettered sequence at right to nail the lath strips — one at a time as you cut them *(Step 3)* — to the panel and to one another with ⅞-inch galvanized-steel brads placed at the ends and at 6-inch intervals in between. First, attach the horizontal and vertical strips marking the outer edges of the trellis and tower, then those marking the inner edges **(A)**. Attach the vertical strips within the trellis and the illusory door **(B)**. Attach the horizontal strips of the door and illusory walkway **(C)**. Attach the diagonal strips of the walkway, trellis and tower **(D)**. For a smooth finish at the top of the tower, nail 2½-inch-long pieces of lath, called mounting blocks, onto the uppermost pair of horizontal strips where they meet the slightly angled tower sides. Finally, nail a second layer of lath to the outer and inner edges of the trellis and to the tower sides **(E)**. ▶

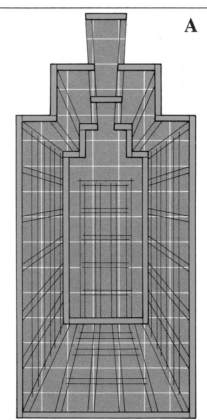

A

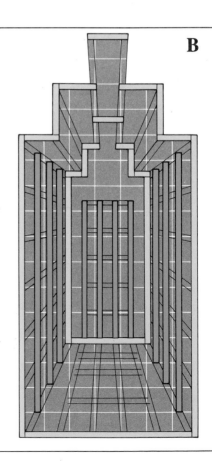

B

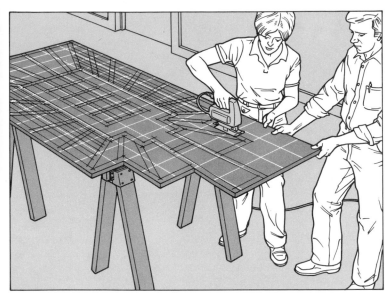

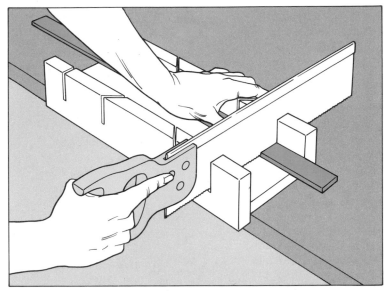

2 **Cutting out the tower pattern.** Fit a saber saw with a ¼-inch plywood blade *(page 122)*, and set the cutting edge of the blade against the upper pencil line four squares from the top at one side of the panel. While a helper holds the corner there to prevent the plywood from splitting, cut along the pencil lines delineating the outer edge of the tower — stopping the saw and starting a new cut from an edge as necessary.

3 **Cutting lath strips.** One strip at a time, measure, mark, cut and nail the lath in the sequence indicated in Step 4, below, beginning with the 1⅜-inch lath that will form parts of the outside frame of the trellis. To prevent the lath from splitting when cut, lay the piece flat in a miter box and push it against the far side, aligning your mark with the 90° slots of the box. Hold the lath tight and cut it with a backsaw *(above)*. The drawings below indicate where horizontal strips butt against vertical ones and vice versa, and thus are a guide to the length of each strip. Add a little extra length to the diagonals so you can trim them easily in Step 5.

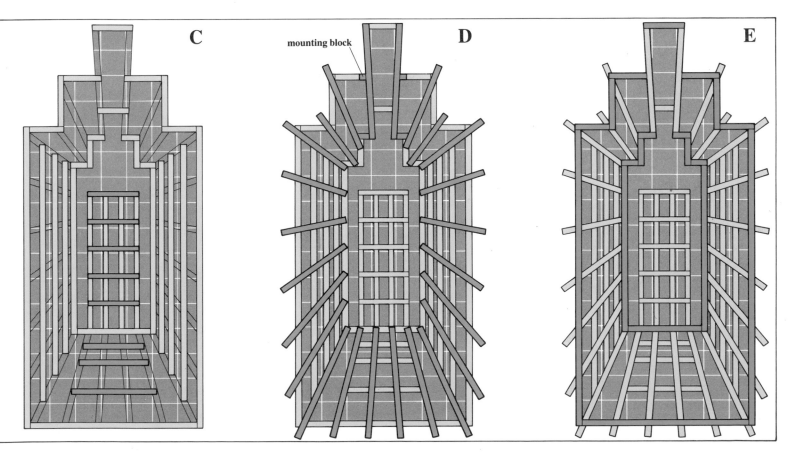

mounting block

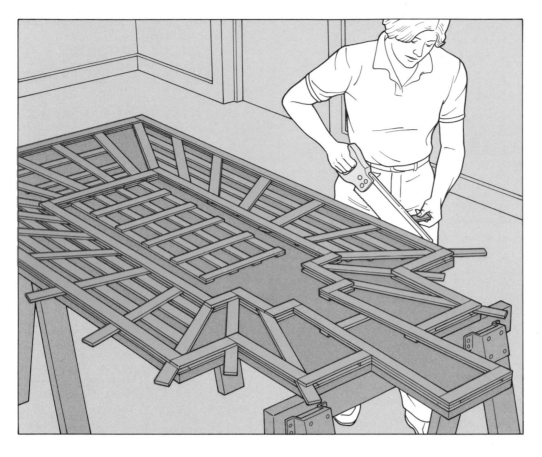

5 **Sawing off exterior lath ends.** Place the backsaw across an overhanging lath, setting the side of the saw blade flush against the edge of the panel. Cut the lath with a single, steady backward stroke, applying light pressure to the saw. Take care not to shave or gouge the panel. Trim all of the other overhanging lath ends similarly.

9 **Mounting the panel.** Stack bricks, concrete blocks or scrap lumber against the fence to form a broad, steady platform 8 inches high where you plan to attach the panel. With the aid of a helper, stand the panel on the platform. Use a carpenter's level to straighten the panel until it is exactly vertical. Then hold the panel in place while your helper drives sixpenny galvanized-steel nails into the plywood at the top corners between the lath (*left*). Then nail the bottom corners and finally drive nails at 2-foot intervals along each side.

6 **Trimming interior lath ends.** Place the blade of a wood chisel across one of the protruding lath ends inside the design. Hold the chisel firmly upright and lightly tap the top of the handle with a hammer until the blade cuts cleanly through the lath. Trim other protruding ends similarly.

7 **Filling gaps.** To conceal a gap where lath strips meet, first place a small glob of vinyl spackling paste on the tip of a putty knife. Carefully force the paste into the gap and draw the knife across the surface to level it. Fill each gap in the same way. Let the spackling paste dry for several hours.

8 **Touching up the paint.** Using a 1-inch nylon brush, coat the exposed exterior ends of lath with white exterior flat latex paint. Before painting the exposed interior edges or the patches of spackling paste, cover the adjacent parts of the panel with masking tape. Let the paint dry for two to three hours before removing the tape.

10 **Extending horizontal strips along the fence.** Approximately 2 inches from each end of a 4-foot-long strip of 1⅜-inch lath, start a ⅞-inch galvanized-steel brad by hammering it partway into the wood. Set the strip on the fence with one end flush against the first angled strip below the tower design of the panel; drive the brad there through the lath and into the fence. Then set the carpenter's level on top of the other end of the lath. Adjust the lath until it is exactly horizontal before driving in the second brad. Repeat this process to attach all of the remaining horizontals.

11 **Nailing intersecting verticals.** Starting at one side of the panel, make tick marks at 1-foot intervals along the top and bottom horizontal lath strips. Align the outside edge of a vertical lath with the set of marks nearest the panel, and nail the lath to the top and bottom strips with ⅞-inch brads. Do the same with the remaining verticals. Then go back and anchor all of the verticals firmly by driving a brad into each intersection.

Providing privacy with a modular screen

Set in a small space, the privacy screen shown below provides a handsome backdrop for the garden and a deft way to separate it from close neighbors without erecting a full fence. The screen's vertical slats, in two alternately spaced rows, permit airflow without sacrificing privacy.

Begin planning the dimensions and location of your screen with a string-and-stake outline *(Step 1)*. Here, the screen is composed of two panels 7 feet wide and 6 feet high, which meet at a 130° angle. But the number, size and relative positions of panels can all be adapted to your site.

Place the screen at least a few inches inside your property line. Local building or zoning authorities can tell you about building-permit and fence-height ordinances that you will need to follow. And talk to neighbors who will share a view of the screen; because it is as attractive from the back as from the front, they may even agree to help in the building.

Your string-and-stake layout will also give you a basis for estimating your lumber needs. This screen is made entirely of pressure-treated yellow pine; even if you choose less expensive wood for the slats and their supports, use pressure-treated posts to prevent belowground rot.

Much of the job can be done by one person, but you will need a helper for some stages. Most of the tools needed are such stand-bys as a garden shovel, hammer, carpenter's level, steel measuring tape, combination square, stepladder and sawhorses. But you will also need two bar clamps, a line level, a circular saw with a crosscut blade and a posthole digger; the bar clamps, saw and digger are available through tool-rental agencies.

The hole made by a posthole digger is much narrower than that dug with a spade, so you need to do less filling and tamping to anchor the posts solidly. To ensure a good foundation for the screen, sink a third of each post belowground — more if the frost line is deeper. Here, the posts rise 6 feet aboveground, requiring 3 feet underground. The hole must always be 4 to 6 inches deeper than the underground part of the post, to allow for gravel and a flat rock below the post *(Step 2)*.

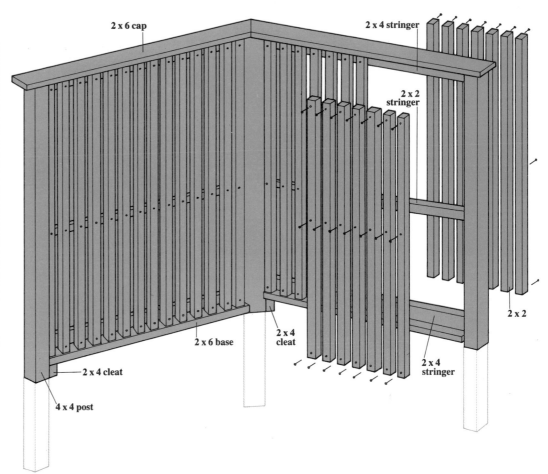

2 x 6 cap

2 x 4 stringer

2 x 2 stringer

2 x 4 cleat

2 x 2

2 x 6 base

2 x 4 cleat

2 x 4 stringer

2 x 4 cleat

4 x 4 post

Materials List

2 x 6	40 ′ pressure-treated yellow pine 2 x 6, cut into 4 cap and base pieces, 10 ′ long
2 x 4	42 ′ pressure-treated yellow pine 2 x 4, cut into: 4 stringers, 10 ′ long 2 cleats, 12 ″ long
4 x 4	30 ′ pressure-treated yellow pine 4 x 4, cut into 3 posts, 10 ′ long
2 x 2	668 ′ pressure-treated yellow pine 2 x 2, cut into: 2 stringers, 10 ′ long 108 slats, 12 ′ long
Nails	3 lbs. tenpenny galvanized-steel common nails

A privacy screen. Vertical slats mounted alternately at the front and back of horizontal stringers add interest — and airiness — to the screen. The stringers are toenailed to the posts supporting the screen; these are anchored by earth packed in holes dug deeper than the frost line. Cleats are used under one end of each base piece to make the panels level even if the ground is not. Caps above the posts and upper stringers keep water out of the end grain of vertical pieces.

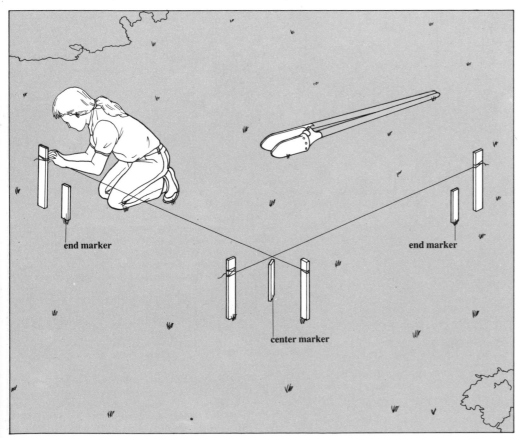

end marker

end marker

center marker

1 Laying out the screen. Drive wood stakes lightly into the ground to mark the ends and center point of the screen. Then drive two taller stakes, one about a foot outside one end of the screen and the other about a foot beyond the center stake, so that a string stretched between the two tall stakes passes directly over the two marker stakes. Similarly set two tall stakes along the line of the other panel, and stretch string between them; the two strings should intersect over the center stake.▶

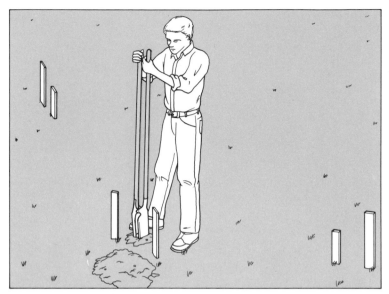

2 x 4 tamper

2 **Digging the postholes.** Remove the strings from the tall stakes. Pull up one of the short marker stakes and use a posthole digger to excavate a hole centered on the position of the stake. To do this, first spread your feet well apart. Grasp both handles of the digger firmly and lift the digger straight up a couple of feet; then plunge the metal spades into the ground. Pulling the handles apart, lift the spades out of the ground, then press the handles together to release the dirt onto a pile near the hole. Dig the hole 3½ feet deep and 8 inches wide at the bottom. Dig similar holes at the positions of the other two marker stakes. Fill the bottom of each hole with 6 inches of gravel topped by a flat stone.

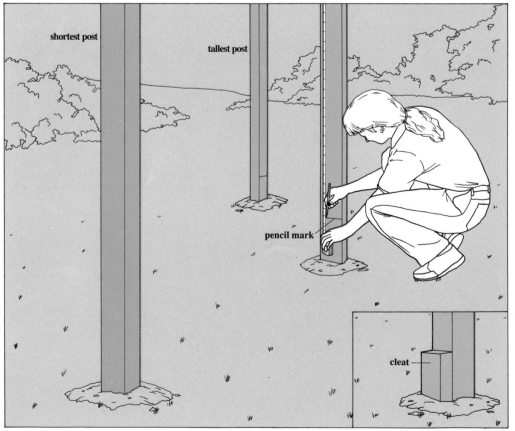

shortest post

tallest post

pencil mark

cleat

5 **Measuring for cleats.** Use a steel tape measure to determine the height of each post from the ground up. If, as in this case, one of the end posts is tallest, measure from the top of that post a distance equal to the height of the center post, and mark this distance on the side of the tall end post that faces the center post. Then compare the heights of the two shorter posts, and mark the inside face of the taller of the two at a distance from the top equal to the height of the shorter. If the center post is the tallest, measure and mark on its side faces distances equal to the heights of the corresponding end posts.

Measure the distance from each mark to the ground, and cut 2-by-4 cleats to match these lengths. Nail the cleats to the inside faces of the posts so that the top of each cleat is level with the pencil mark and its bottom is touching the ground (*inset*).

3 **Putting in the first post.** Stretch the strings between the tall stakes again, then slide a 4-by-4 post into one of the end holes. Position the post so its back face is flush with the string, then hold a carpenter's level against the front face of the post, adjusting the post until it is vertical. Have a helper shovel a few inches of dirt into the hole and tamp it firmly with a 2-by-4 *(left)*, to provide some support for the post. Move the level to an adjacent face of the post, again adjusting the post until it is vertical. Have your helper fill the hole with dirt, tamping it firm after every couple of shovelfuls. As the hole is filled, regularly check the two adjacent faces with the level, adjusting the post as required.

4 **Adjusting post heights.** Slide a post into the center hole, holding it upright so the corners of its back face touch the crossed strings at points equidistant from the strings' intersection *(inset)*. Drive a small nail lightly into the front faces of both posts, 1 inch from the top, and stretch a string between the two nails. Suspend a line level on the string, and have your helper read the level as you hold the center post upright. If the string is not level, indicating that the top of the center post is too high or too low, remove the post from its hole and adjust the level of the gravel below the flat stone as required. When the string between the posts is level, remove it and follow the instructions in Step 3 to plumb and stabilize the center post. Repeat this procedure to set the third post.

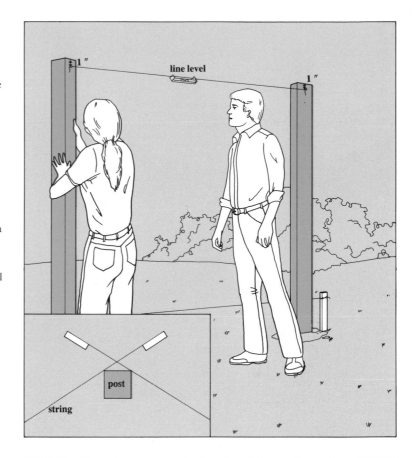

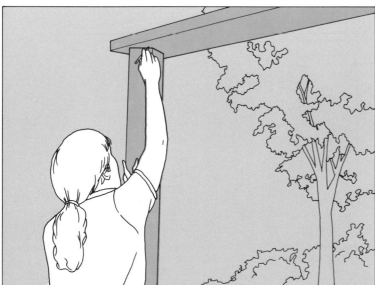

6 **Marking a base piece.** Lay a 2-by-6 across the tops of an end post and the center post. Let its ends extend beyond the post tops and its edges overhang the posts equally on each side. Pencil a line on the underside of the 2-by-6 where it meets the inner face of the center post at an angle. Scribe a similar line on the 2-by-6 where it meets the inner face of the end post *(above)*; this line should be perpendicular to the 2-by-6's long edges. Take the 2-by-6 down and use a straightedge to extend each of the lines to the edges of the board. With a circular saw *(page 123)*, cut the board inside the lines. Mark the angle of the center post on another 2-by-6; make sure its other end overhangs the end post by at least 5 inches. Cut along the line, then set the board aside for use later as the cap piece.

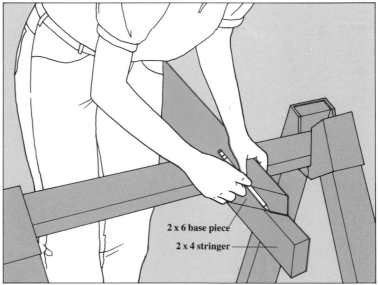

7 **Marking the stringers.** Set a 2-by-4 stringer on edge on a flat surface. Place the cut 2-by-6 base piece atop the 2-by-4 so that a few inches of the lower board protrude at each end. Position the top board so that one edge is flush with one side of the stringer; you may need help holding the larger board in place. Pencil onto the 2-by-4 the angles at the ends of the 2-by-6. Repeat this procedure for another 2-by-4 and a 2-by-2, then use the circular saw to cut these stringers inside these lines. ▶

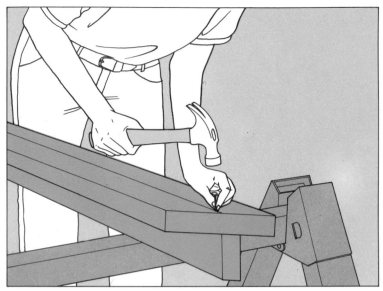

8 **Assembling the bottom pieces.** Draw a pencil line along the center of the wide bottom face of the 2-by-6 base piece. Put the 2-by-6 on top of the narrow face of the bottom stringer so that the angled ends are flush and the edges of the 2-by-6 overhang the 2-by-4 by an equal amount on each side. Drive a tenpenny galvanized-steel nail into the line about 2 inches from the angled end. Hold the 2-by-6 firmly as you drive the nail through it into the 2-by-4. Drive more nails along the line at 12-inch intervals, checking the positions of the boards as you go.

9 **Attaching the bottom assembly.** Invert the T-shaped assembly, and slip it into place between the two posts, resting one end on the ground, the other end on a cleat. Center the 2-by-6 on the cleated post, then drive two tenpenny nails through the 2-by-6 into the cleat, about 1 inch from the post. Attach the opposite end of the assembly to the other post by toenailing — driving a nail at an angle through the top of the 2-by-4 stringer, then driving nails at an angle through each side of the 2-by-4.

TIP: To simplify toenailing, start the first nail before putting the assembly in place. Start the nail tip into the 2-by-4 an inch from the end; push the nail to a 45° angle and drive it until the tip protrudes from the end grain. Finish driving the nail when the assembly is in place.

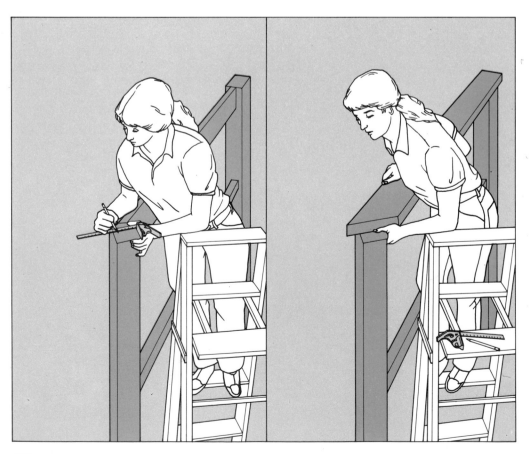

11 **Marking for the cap piece.** At the top of the center post, mark the middle of the front face, then use a combination square to make a line from this mark across the center of the post top (*far left*). Position the angled end of the 2-by-6 cap piece on this line (*near left*), and center the angled end over the post and the top stringer. At the square end of the cap piece, measure and mark a 2-inch overhang beyond the end post. Cut a square end on the cap piece at this mark. Set the piece aside.

Now repeat Steps 6 through 10 to assemble and attach the base piece and stringers for the screen's other panel. When they are fixed in place, mark and cut the cap piece for that panel as you did the one for the first panel.

10 **Toenailing the top stringer.** Lift the 2-by-4 top stringer into position between the two posts, centered between the edges of the posts and with its narrow face flush with the post tops. While your helper holds the stringer in place, drive two nails through the point of the angled end into the post *(right)*. Attach the other end of the stringer by toenailing through the bottom of the stringer. Attach the 2-by-2 stringer in the same manner, midway between the top and bottom stringers.

12 **Nailing the cap piece.** Draw a center line along the top of each cap piece as a guide for nailing, then position one cap piece over its posts and top stringer. Carefully align the angled end with the pencil line on the center post, then drive tenpenny nails at 12-inch intervals along the guideline, through the 2-by-6 cap piece into the posts and the stringer. Attach the other cap piece in the same manner.

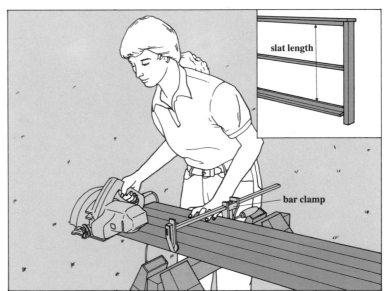

slat length

bar clamp

13 **Cutting the vertical slats.** Determine the length of the vertical slats by measuring the distance from the bottom of the cap piece to the top of the base piece on one panel *(inset)*. Lay several 2-by-2s across the work surface with their ends even, then clamp them firmly together with a pair of bar clamps, positioned about 2 feet from each end. Mark the length of the vertical slats across the width of the clamped 2-by-2s, then cut along the line with a circular saw. Continue clamping, marking and cutting 2-by-2 slats until you have enough to cover the panel; the number of slats equals half the distance, in inches, between the two posts. Measure the slat length for the other panel of the screen, and mark and cut its slats. ▶

107

A wood shield to

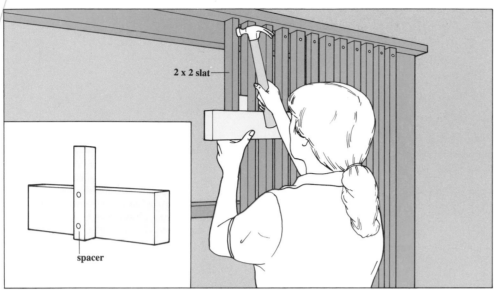

14 **Nailing the slats.** To help position the slats as you nail them, make a spacer by nailing a 2-by-2 across a 2-by-4, with one end of the 2-by-2 flush with one edge of the 2-by-4 *(inset)*. Hold the spacer near the top of one end post, with the 2-by-2 against the post's inside face. Set a slat snugly against the other side of the spacer with its back face against the top stringer. Drive a tenpenny nail through the slat into the stringer. Move the spacer to the bottom of the end post, and nail the slat to the bottom stringer; then nail it to the middle stringer. Attach successive slats — using the spacer in the same way — until you reach about 18 inches from the center post.

15 **Adjusting slat intervals.** Lay out each of the remaining slats perpendicular to the screen, with one end on the ground and the other end resting on the base piece. Adjust the slats until the intervals between them are equal, then use a pencil to mark lines on the base piece on each side of each slat. Set the first slat on end between its marks, and nail it to the bottom stringer; use a level to make sure it is vertical before nailing it to the top stringer. Attach the remaining slats in the same way. Then nail slats to the other side of the screen, positioning them so they are opposite the gaps between the front slats. Finally, attach slats to the other panel of the screen.

Modular wood shields that further simplify the design of the privacy screen on the preceding pages are an easy answer to the problem of concealing trash cans, mulch piles and such. In fact, the shields can actually enhance landscaping: Plants and flowers go beautifully against a natural-finish or painted wood backdrop.

The shield at right is made of pressure-treated pine and is specifically tailored to hide an air-conditioning unit located in the corner of a fenced-in flagstone patio. The shield consists of two identical panels, each slightly more than 4 feet wide and 3½ feet tall.

Panel dimensions, of course, can be modified. Or, if the eyesore is located alongside a fence, a wall or the house instead of in a corner, a third panel can be added. The panels are joined by rust-resistant butt hinges and can be attached to any wood surface with hooks and screw eyes. Both the hinges, which are sold with matching screws, and the hook and screw-eye units are available at hardware stores.

Each panel consists of a frame of 2-by-4s faced with 1-by-6s, nailed alternately to the front and back. The open design allows air to circulate through the panels — an important consideration when you are hiding a cooling unit that needs to breathe to operate effectively.

One person can build the shield, working with basic tools — a hammer, awl, screwdriver, tape measure, pliers and backsaw — on any comfortably large and flat work space, such as a driveway or garage floor.

Once the shield has been assembled, the pressure-treated pine can be left to weather naturally. So, too, can redwood or cedar. If you wish to paint or stain pressure-treated pine, let it weather for at least six months to allow the treatment substances to dry thoroughly; then coat the pine with a finish designed for exterior use. If you build a shield out of less expensive untreated pine, apply a wood preservative immediately.

hide backyard eyesores

Materials List

2 x 4	30 ′ pressure-treated yellow pine 2 x 4, cut into: 4 frame sides, 42 ″ long 4 frame tops and bottoms, 46½ ″ long
1 x 6	41 ′ pressure-treated yellow pine 1 x 6, cut into: 18 facing boards, 38 ″ long 2 cap pieces, 49½ ″ long
Hardware	2 rust-resistant 2½ ″ butt hinges screws included 2 screen-door hook and screw-eye units ½ lb. tenpenny galvanized-steel common nails 1 lb. sixpenny galvanized-steel common nails

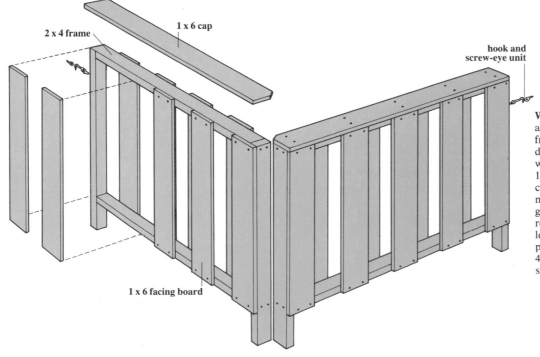

Wood shield. Nailing 1-by-6 facing boards alternately to the front and back of 2-by-4 frames gives this simple wood shield a decorative flair. The frame is put together with tenpenny galvanized-steel nails; the 1-by-6 facing boards and cap pieces are secured with sixpenny galvanized-steel nails. To allow the hinges to close at a 90° angle, a tiny triangle is sawed off the right rear corner of the cap on one panel and the left rear corner of the cap on the other panel. Hook and screw-eye units on the 2-by-4 uprights at opposite ends of the frame secure the shield to a wood surface.

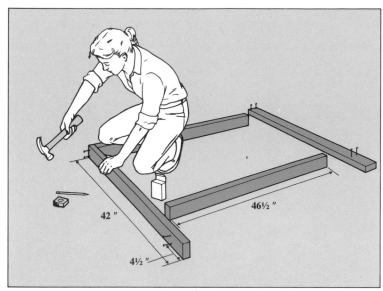

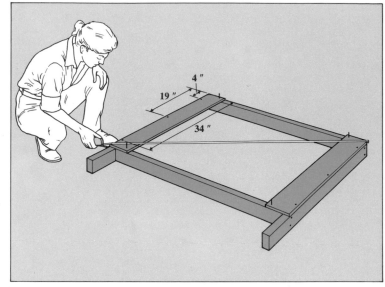

1 **Making the frame.** Using a pencil and steel tape measure, make tick marks for nails 1 inch from each edge of two 42-inch 2-by-4s — putting marks ¾ inch from one end and 4½ inches from the other end of each board. Drive tenpenny galvanized-steel nails partway into the boards at the marked positions. Lay one of these 42-inch 2-by-4s on edge, and butt one end of a 46½-inch board against it, as shown above. Bracing the longer board with your knee and holding the short one with your hand, drive in the pair of nails at that end. Butt the end of a second 46½-inch 2-by-4 opposite the second set of started nails on the 42-inch board and drive in the nails. Finally, align the other 42-inch 2-by-4 with the unattached ends of the 46½-inch boards and drive in the nails.

2 **Squaring the frame.** Align two 38-inch 1-by-6 boards flush with the top and the side edges of the frame. Make marks for nails 4, 19 and 34 inches from the tops of the boards and ¾ inch from the outside edges. Make two other marks for nails ¾ inch from the top and bottom ends and 1½ inches from the inside edges. Start sixpenny galvanized-steel nails partway into the boards at all the marks. Realign the 1-by-6s and drive in the nails along the outside edges. Stretch a steel tape measure diagonally from corner to corner in first one, then the other direction. If the diagonals are not equal, gently tap the top corner of the 42-inch 2-by-4 that is at the end of the longest measurement until the diagonals are equal. Then drive in the four remaining nails to secure the frame.

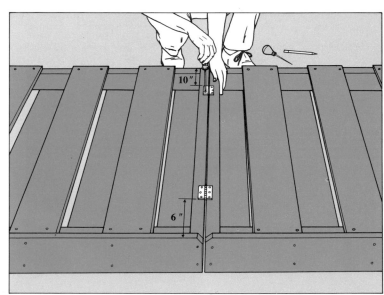

5 **Sawing off an inside corner.** Stand a panel upright. Working from the back of the panel at the corner where the panels will be joined, make marks ¾ inch from the corner. Connect the marks with a straight line. Use a backsaw to cut off the corner (above). Do the same to the appropriate corner of the other panel. These cuts will allow the hinged panels to close at a 90° angle to each other.

6 **Attaching the hinges.** Lay the panels side by side, backs upward, leaving about ¼ inch between them. Place rust-resistant butt hinges on the panels with the ¼-inch-wide knuckles of each hinge directly over the space between the panels. Locate the top of one hinge 6 inches from the panel cap and the bottom of the other hinge 10 inches from the bottom of the panels. Holding each hinge in place, make tick marks through the hinge holes for the accompanying screws. Start the holes with an awl. Place a screw in each hinge hole and tighten with a screwdriver.

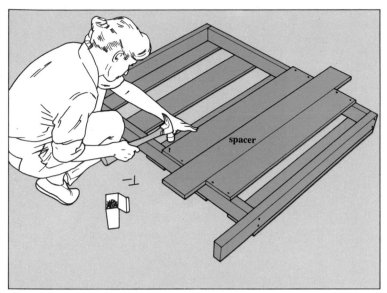

3 **Fastening the facing boards.** Mark nail holes 1½ inches from each side and ¾ inch from the top and bottom of the seven remaining 1-by-6 facing boards for this panel. Start sixpenny galvanized-steel nails at all the marks. To align each facing board correctly, use a 49½-inch 1-by-6 as a spacer. Place the spacer alongside a nailed corner 1-by-6 on the front of the frame. Align a facing board alongside the spacer and drive in the nails. Nail the other two front boards in the same way. Then turn the frame over and place the spacer along a vertical frame edge. Align a 1-by-6 facing board alongside the spacer and drive in the nails. Nail the three remaining boards in the same way.

4 **Attaching the panel cap.** Measure and mark for nails ¾ inch from each end and 2 inches from each edge of a 49½-inch 1-by-6. Mark for additional pairs of nails at 12-inch intervals between the end marks. Start sixpenny galvanized-steel nails at the marks. Turn the frame over so that the front is again facing up. Working on a flat surface to help align the cap flush with the back of the frame, drive the end nails into the 42-inch 2-by-4 uprights. Then drive in the remaining nails. Repeat Steps 1 through 4 to assemble the other panel.

7 **Hanging the screen.** Stand the screen upright around the air-conditioning unit with the free sides abutting adjacent sides of the fence. Working from inside the screen with an awl, start a screw hole in the edge of one 2-by-4 about 10 inches from its top corner. Screw the hook of a hook and screw-eye unit into the hole, using pliers if need be to tighten it securely. Extend the hook to the fence, and mark the proper location for the screw eye with a pencil (right). Start a hole with the awl at the mark, screw the eye into the fence and attach the hook. Follow the same procedure to hang the other panel.

Gingerbread cutouts for a touch of Victoriana

Plain wood-frame screen doors can evoke the charms of an earlier era when they are trimmed with gingerbread, the ornate wood scrollwork that Victorians delighted in using to decorate the exteriors of their homes. This door's panels are trimmed with brackets and spindles, designs you can easily reproduce with the help of a grid *(Step 1)*. But other gingerbread patterns are just as simple to create *(page 115),* and all can easily be cut from ½-inch-thick exterior-grade plywood with a saber saw and then sanded for a perfect fit.

The cutout designs at right are scaled to fit this particular door — a widely available model with a fairly common arrangement and spacing of its wood framework elements. If your door is built to a different pattern, you can adapt the designs to fit it by taking measurements and experimenting on the grid paper *(Step 1)*. In order for you to be able to nail the ½-inch-thick cutouts in place, the wood framework of your door should be at least ½ inch thick on the side of the screen where the trim is being added. Before beginning the project, pull out the door's hinge pins and remove it from the jamb.

You will need about 4 square feet of the plywood, a 7-by-11-inch piece of lightweight cardboard or heavy paper on which to draw the grid, 1 quart of satin exterior enamel, a roll of 2-inch-wide masking tape to protect the screen while you paint its wood frame, ½ pound of fourpenny galvanized-steel finishing nails, exterior spackle to touch up the nail holes and a few sheets of coarse (60-grit) and medium (100-grit) sandpaper.

In addition to the saber saw, you will need a few other tools: either scissors or a utility knife to cut out the cardboard patterns, C clamps to hold the plywood board in position as you cut out the gingerbread, a ½-inch-wide fine-bristled angled paintbrush, a 2-inch-wide standard paintbrush, a tack hammer, a nail set, a putty knife and a power drill. Although you can manage without it, a 1½-inch-diameter sanding drum that fits on the power drill will speed the sanding process, especially in the gingerbread's hard-to-get-at inside curves.

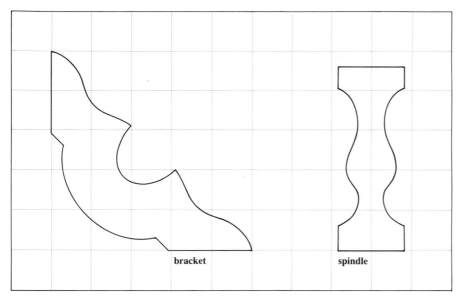

bracket   spindle

1 **Making the patterns.** Draw a grid of 1-inch squares on a 7-by-11-inch piece of lightweight cardboard or heavy paper. Make tick marks on your cardboard grid at every point where the outlines of the bracket and spindle pieces cross the lines of this grid. Connect the marks, using a ruler for the straight lines and a compass or the bottom of a glass or bottle to guide your pencil around curves. Cut out the patterns with scissors or a utility knife. Check the patterns against your door; if they do not fit, experiment on grid paper until you achieve designs of the proper size.

2 **Transferring the patterns to wood.** Set the bracket pattern on a 2-foot-square, ½-inch-thick piece of exterior-grade plywood. Trace around the edge of the pattern with a pencil. Draw 18 brackets on the plywood board, leaving at least ¼ inch of space between them. To make cutting them out easier, all of the brackets should face in the same direction. You need only 16 brackets, but trace two extra in case you spoil any while cutting them. Then place the spindle pattern on the plywood. Trace it four times, allowing one extra spindle in case of a cutting error.

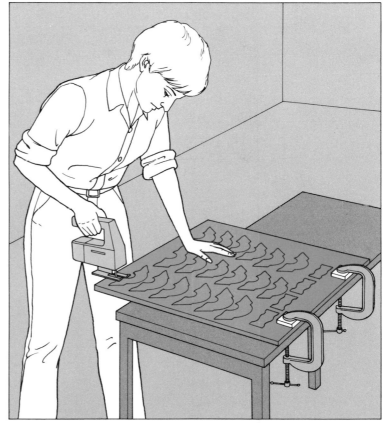

3 **Cutting out the pieces.** Position the marked board so that a row of out-lined brackets hangs over the edge of the worktable. Clamp the board in place with two C clamps, fitting a wood scrap between each clamp and the board to protect the wood's surface. Cut out the brackets one at a time with a saber saw, using a ¼-inch-wide plywood-cutting blade *(page 122):* Begin by sawing from the edge of the board to cut out a brack-et's semicircle *(above).* Because it is impossible to make a sharp turn with a saber saw, saw back to the edge of the board as necessary and start a new cut in order to complete a sharp corner. Steady the piece with your hand as you near the end of a cutting line. Shift and reclamp the board as needed to cut out the remaining pieces. ▶

masking tape

4 **Sanding and fitting the cutouts.** Smooth the edges of each cutout with coarse (60-grit) sandpaper. Then finish the edges and flat surfaces with medium (100-grit) sandpaper. When sanding edges that will fit against the door's framework, check periodically to see that the piece fits snugly (*above*). After you have test-fitted each piece, lay it on newspaper in the same position in which it will appear on the door.

5 **Painting the door and cutouts.** Place the door on one of its side edges against the wall atop a protective covering of newspaper. Stick strips of 2-inch-wide masking tape over both sides of the screen next to the wood frame. Paint the door's top and bottom edges with satin exterior enamel, using a 2-inch-wide brush. After the paint has dried, turn the door upright and paint the side edges. Next, paint the inside edges of the frame, using a ½-inch-wide angled brush. Then use the 2-inch-wide brush to paint the frame itself — first the horizontal sections, then the vertical (*above*). When the paint is dry, turn the door over and do the other side. Paint the edges of the cutouts with the angled brush. Then do the flat surfaces, one side at a time, with the other brush. Let the paint dry.

7 **Nailing cutouts to the door.** Position a bracket in the appropriate corner of the frame. Insert fourpenny galvanized-steel finishing nails through the drilled holes, and hammer the nails into place with a tack hammer. Then drive the head of each nail slightly below the wood's surface using a nail set (*left*). Turn the door as you work so that you are always hammering downward. Position and attach the spindles in a similar fashion, putting one spindle in the center of the door and the other two spindles just under the gap between the brackets. Finally, fill each nail hole with exterior spackle. Smooth away the excess with a putty knife. After the spackle has dried, sand lightly with medium (100-grit) sandpaper and touch up the wood using the ½-inch-wide brush. The door is now ready to be hung.

6 **Drilling nail holes.** On a flat side of each bracket piece, measure for and mark lines ½ inch and 1½ inches from each end. Extend the lines, perpendicular to the flat side, onto the curved edges of the piece. Put scrap wood under the bracket; then, at the center of each extended line, drill a hole straight down through the curved edge with a $\frac{1}{16}$-inch bit *(right)*. Let the bit go all the way through the bracket. On each spindle piece, measure for and mark a line ¼ inch from each side along each of the spindle's four inside curves. Put a piece of scrap wood under the spindle, and drill a hole downward through the center of each line at a steep angle — about 70° — so that the bit comes through the spindle's end *(inset)*.

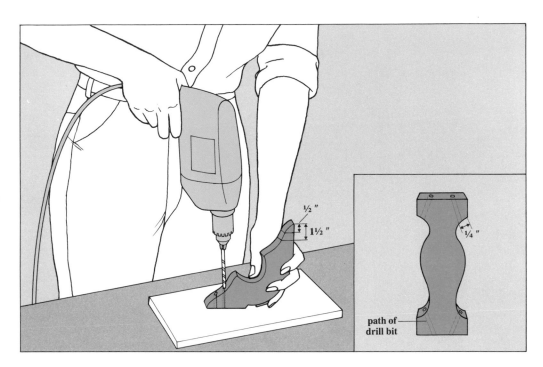

More Gingerbread Designs

These three additional patterns for gingerbread cutouts can also be made by transferring them to 1-inch-square grid paper and following the instructions that begin on page 113. If you want to make the brackets shown on the center door below, you will need a 1-inch-diameter spade bit to drill the circular holes. Sand the holes with a sanding drum or a piece of medium (100-grit) sandpaper wrapped around your finger. If you prefer to create your own patterns, begin by drawing them on graph paper. Then cut them out and fit them on a miniature door drawn to scale to see how they look.

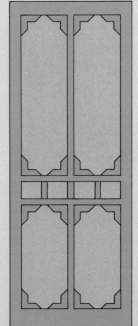

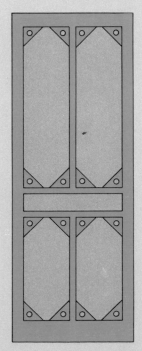

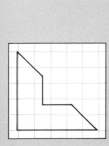

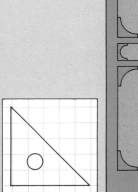

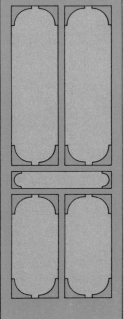

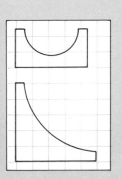

A porch shade for privacy and protection

Open porches are summer's living rooms — places to entertain, picnic, relax in a rocker, enjoy a cooling breeze. By adding a colorful shade like the one at left, you can enjoy a roll-up, roll-down fabric wall that provides privacy as well as protection from the sun's glare or a sudden shower.

The shade's fabric is awning material: durable and tightly woven 100 per cent acrylic fibers, which repel water and resist mildew. Available from awning companies or boating-supply stores, the fabric comes in a range of vibrant colors that will not fade, even after prolonged exposure to the sun. Because acrylic fabrics are only 31 inches or 46 inches wide, you will need to sew several panels together to make a broad shade *(page 118)*. Unlike most outdoor fabrics, this material is relatively light, weighing only 9½ ounces per square yard; a home sewing machine can easily stitch it. Furthermore, the fabric has no wrong or right side.

Rods inserted into casings at top and bottom keep the shade smooth. The bottom rod must be heavy to hold down the shade; steel pipe will do the job. If your shade is less than 15 feet wide select a pipe 1 inch in diameter; shades between 15 and 24 feet wide require a 1¼-inch pipe. Have the pipe cut ¼ inch shorter than the finished width of the shade so that its ends will not stick out. A ¼-inch-diameter rod of lightweight fiberglass is adequate for the top, although you can use a steel pipe there, too, if necessary.

Head-rod clips — metal clips with C-shaped openings to clasp the rod — suspend the shade from its screw-hook mountings. The clips, which should be ⅛ inch larger in diameter than the rod, have hooks from which pulleys for the draw cord are hung. Choose single pulleys with grooved wheels that can hold ³⁄₁₆-inch-thick braided nylon rope. To figure how much rope you need, multiply the shade's length by six. Fiberglass rods, steel pipes, rope, pulleys and head-rod clips can be purchased at awning shops, and some of the items are available at building-supply stores and plumbing dealers.

The materials listed at right yield a shade 8 feet 4 inches long and 6 feet 7 inches wide. When adjusting the amount of fabric for a larger or smaller shade, add 7¼ inches to the desired finished length for rod casings and 5 inches to the desired finished width for side hems.

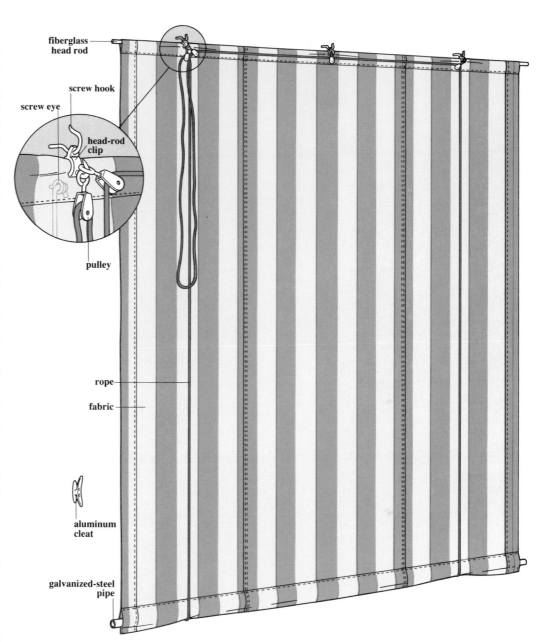

fiberglass head rod

screw hook

screw eye

head-rod clip

pulley

rope

fabric

aluminum cleat

galvanized-steel pipe

Materials List	
Fabric	9 yards 100% acrylic fabric, 31 ″ wide, cut into 3 panels 108 ″ (3 yards) long
Hardware	1 fiberglass rod, ¼ ″ in diameter, 6 ′6¾ ″ long
	1 galvanized-steel pipe, 1 ″ in diameter, 6 ′6¾ ″ long
	3 aluminum head-rod clips, ⅜ ″ in diameter
	4 single aluminum pulleys, 1½ ″ long
	1 aluminum cleat, 4½ ″ long, with wood screw
	3 screw hooks, ³⁄₁₆ ″ in diameter, 1½ ″ long
	2 screw eyes, ³⁄₁₆ ″ in diameter, 1½ ″ long
Rope	50 ′ braided nylon rope, ³⁄₁₆ ″ thick

A roll-up shade. Three widths of 31-inch acrylic fabric are sewed together and hemmed on each side to form this extra-wide shade. The fiberglass rod, from which the shade hangs, rests in a casing sewed into the top; a heavy, galvanized-steel pipe in a casing on the bottom keeps the fabric taut. (Here, both rods are shown protruding from their casings; in reality they should be shorter so their ends are hidden.) Three head-rod clips — metal fasteners that grip the fabric-encased top rod — hang from hooks screwed into the porch fascia. The shade is raised or lowered by a nylon rope knotted at each end to a screw eye. The rope traverses small pulleys that hang from the rod clips. Its draw loop is secured to a V-shaped cleat screwed into a wall.

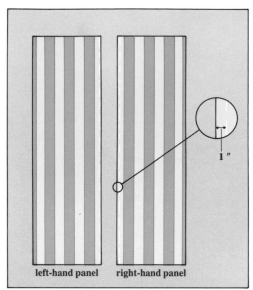

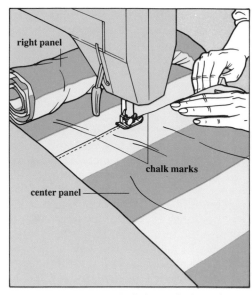

1 **Marking the porch fascia.** Pencil a mark on the fascia where you wish the top of the shade to be. Obtain a level reading on a carpenter's level held against the mark, then use the level as a straightedge to draw a faint horizontal line *(above)* as long as the desired shade width. Measure from the line to the floor to determine the shade's length. Cut panels of fabric — in this case, three panels are used — to form one large sheet wide enough to make the shade.

2 **Marking fabric panels.** Spread one fabric panel flat on a large table. From the panel's right-hand edge, measure 1 inch toward the left, and mark lightly with chalk. Working lengthwise, continue measuring and marking 1 inch from the right edge. This piece of fabric will form the left-hand panel of the shade. Spread another length of fabric flat and measure 1 inch from the left edge. Mark the entire length of fabric. This will be the shade's right-hand panel.

3 **Attaching panels.** Roll the marked panels lengthwise, leaving the chalk marks visible. Slide the top of the right-hand panel under the sewing machine's arm. Align the right edge of the unmarked panel with the chalk marks. Sew the panels together ¼ inch from the center panel's edge. To avoid puckering, pull the right-hand panel taut as you sew. Add a second row of stitches ¼ inch from the first. Now attach the left-hand panel in the same way.

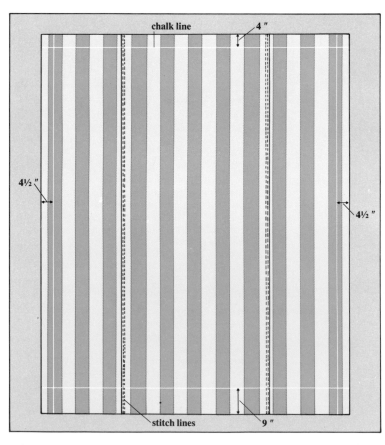

5 **Marking casings and hems.** Unfold the fabric. Draw chalk marks 4 inches from the top edge. Connect the marks with a straight line. This section of the fabric will form the 1¾-inch head-rod casing and its ½-inch turn-under. Next, draw chalk marks 9 inches from the bottom edge and connect them with a straight line. This section will form the 4-inch bottom-rod casing and its 1-inch turn-under. First at the left-hand edge of the fabric, then at the right-hand edge, mark the side hems by chalking marks 4½ inches from the edge and connecting them with a straight line.

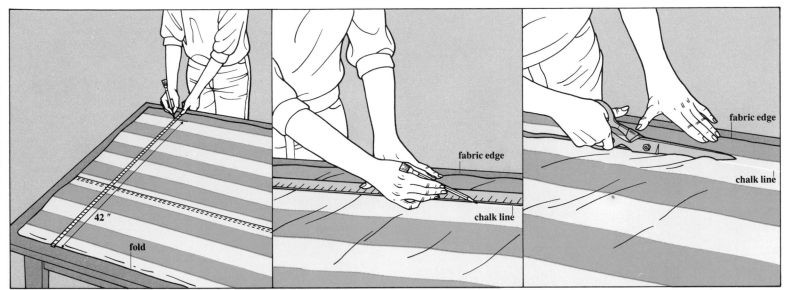

4 **Trimming the fabric.** Spread the fabric flat on a large table and fold it in half lengthwise. Measure the fabric from the fold to ½ the unfinished width of the shade — in this case, 42 inches. Mark this point with chalk (*above, left*), and continue measuring and marking along the

fabric until the marks parallel the full length of the folded edge. With a straightedge, draw a chalk line connecting all the marks (*above, center*). Then trim off the excess material by cutting along the chalk line with a pair of sharp scissors (*above, right*).

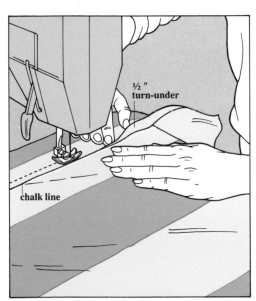

6 **Sewing side hems.** Slide one of the side edges under the sewing-machine needle. Fold over the cut edge ½ inch to make a turn-under. Fold again to bring the first folded edge even with the chalk line. Stitch the folded edge and turn-under in place ¼ inch from the inside folded edge. Then sew a second row of stitches ⅛ inch from the outside folded edge. Stitch the other side hem in the same way.

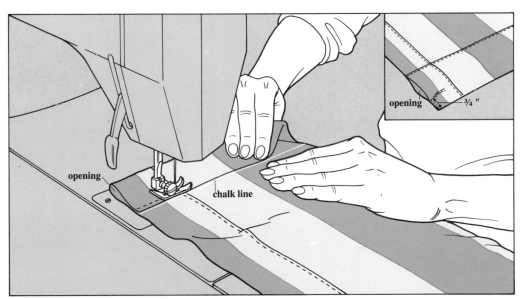

7 **Sewing rod casings.** At the top edge of the shade, fold over ½ inch of fabric to make a turn-under. Fold again to bring the edge flush with the chalk line. As you sew the folded edge in place (*above*), make sure to line up the stripes and keep the ½-inch turn-under beneath the fold. Sew the bottom casing in the same way, but tuck under 1 inch instead of ½ inch. Next, position one of the bottom casing's openings under the needle. Starting from the fold and ⅛ inch from the side edge, close off part of the casing by sewing a ¾-inch-long row of stitches parallel to the side edge (*inset*); the stitches will prevent the steel pipe from slipping out of the casing. Go over the stitches several times for reinforcement. Seal the opposite end of the casing in the same way. ▶

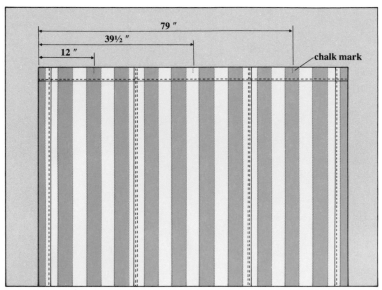

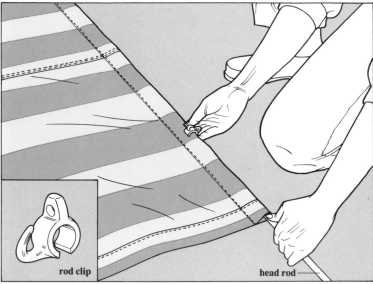

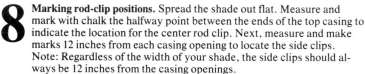

8 **Marking rod-clip positions.** Spread the shade out flat. Measure and mark with chalk the halfway point between the ends of the top casing to indicate the location for the center rod clip. Next, measure and make marks 12 inches from each casing opening to locate the side clips. Note: Regardless of the width of your shade, the side clips should always be 12 inches from the casing openings.

9 **Inserting the head rod.** Turn a rod clip *(inset)* with its hook facing up, and slide it onto the top casing at one of the chalk marks. Position the other two rod clips at the other chalk marks. Then insert the fiberglass rod into the casing, passing it through the C-shaped opening of each clip.

10 **Hanging the shade.** Mark with a pencil the midpoint of the horizontal line drawn on the porch fascia in Step 1. Locate and mark points on the line 12 inches from each end, then make two more marks ½ inch below each of those two. Now, using a ⅛-inch twist bit, drill pilot holes about 1 inch deep at the marked positions. Twist a screw hook into each of the three holes on top and a screw eye into the two bottom holes. If you cannot twist them all the way in by hand, use a screwdriver slipped through the hook or eye as a lever. Finally, while a helper steadies one end of the shade *(left),* slip the rod clips on the top casing over the screw hooks. Make sure that the hook portion of the rod clips faces the inside of the porch.

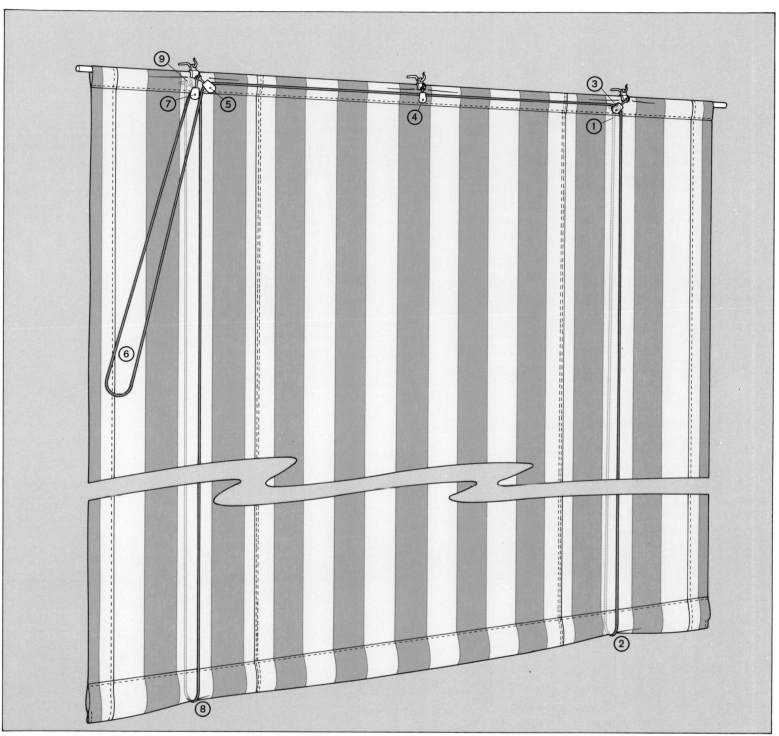

11 **Threading the pulleys.** Hang a pulley on the hook of each rod clip. Add a second pulley to the left rod clip to accommodate the shade's pull cord. Working at the rear of the shade, slip one end of the rope into the right screw eye (**1**) and tie off with a firm knot. Drop the rest of the rope down the back of the shade, bring it around the bottom and up the front (**2**). From right to left, feed the rope through the wheel of the right-hand pulley (**3**). Then feed the rope from right to left through the center pulley (**4**), and through one of the two pulleys (**5**) on the left rod clip. Pull enough rope through (about 10 feet) to make a long loop (**6**) for the pull cord. Then thread the remaining pulley (**7**) left to right and drop the rope down the front of the shade (**8**). Bring the rope around the bottom and up the back. Feed the rope through the left-hand screw eye (**9**) and pull it straight. Tie a knot around the screw eye and cut off the excess rope. Finally, insert the galvanized-steel pipe into the bottom-rod casing. The shade can now be raised and lowered.

Tools for outdoor projects

Working on a project outdoors can be a pleasant change from working in the basement or garage. And making a few preparations can guarantee that your open-air shop will be as productive as an indoor one.

The first requirement is to provide a flat surface where you can cut or assemble pieces of your project. Sturdy sawhorses, made with 2-by-4s and fastened with heavy-duty galvanized-steel brackets, provide a steady base. Spanning the sawhorses with planks or plywood creates a convenient worktable.

If you will be using power tools, get extension cords long enough to reach to an outlet with inches to spare. Except for double-insulated power tools, which work from a two-prong plug system, most tools have three-prong plugs, which are grounded to your household power system to protect you against electric shock — an essential consideration when working outdoors. Moist earth and hands increase the risk of shock in the event of a short circuit in a tool or cord. Never use power tools in rainy or damp weather, even with grounded plugs and outlets.

The specific tools you need will vary, of course, with your project. In general, inferior tools produce inferior work; when buying shop tools, pass by the cheapest ones. Look for such features as permanently lubricated bearings, which simplify tool maintenance, and double-insulated plastic bodies, which eliminate the need for a grounded electric outlet. For heavy-duty work like deck building and masonry cutting, aluminum-housed tools are more durable; they come with three-prong plugs for grounded outlets.

Just as important as buying the right tools is using the right tool for the job. A saber saw, for example, is designed for cutting curves *(below);* although it can make a long, straight cut through plywood, the straight cut will be cleaner and more precise if done with a circular saw *(opposite).* All power tools come with instructions. Take the time to read these, then practice before you begin a project.

Safety is as important as skill, and a few rules apply in every situation:

- Dress for the job. Avoid loose clothing, tuck in your shirt, and roll up your sleeves. Tie back long hair. Wear goggles when there is a chance that sawdust will fly into your eyes. Do not wear gloves when using power tools; gloves reduce dexterity and can catch in moving parts.
- When operating a power tool, be sure to work on a stable surface; with wood or masonry projects, clamp materials to the surface whenever practical.
- Stand comfortably, do not reach any farther than you easily can, and never stand directly in front of — or directly behind — a moving saw blade. Circular saws tend to kick back toward the operator if the blade gets jammed in the middle of a cut; this generally happens when the sawed section has not been supported as it ought to be to let the saw blade move freely. If the blade should bind, switch the saw off immediately and support the work to open the cut. For long cuts, recruit a helper to support the board.
- Always unplug power tools when they are not being used and whenever you adjust or change parts.

The Saber Saw

Because the blade of a saber saw is only about ¼ inch wide, it can be maneuvered through tight spots and intricate, curved cuts without binding or breaking. With straight cuts, the narrow blade tends to wander from a guideline. But a straightedge guide clamped to the work *(opposite, bottom)* will help keep such cuts on line.

Your best buy is a variable-speed saw that you can speed up along broad curves and slow down for tricky areas. Blades come in sets and individually. Most will cut through wood up to 2 inches thick. Blades with six teeth per inch make fast, rough cuts; blades with 10 to 14 teeth per inch cut more slowly, but also more cleanly. For fine cuts in plywood, buy taper-ground blades with 10 teeth per inch.

To ensure a smooth cut on the good face of a board or panel, work with that surface down. The saber-saw blade cuts on the upstroke, sometimes tearing slivers from the top surface of the work.

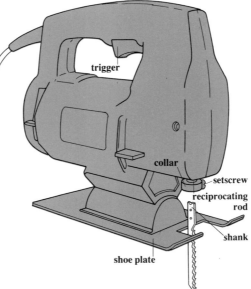

A variable-speed saber saw. A trigger in the handle lets you turn the saw on and off and regulate the speed with which it cuts. To insert a blade, loosen the setscrew in the collar on the reciprocating rod with a screwdriver or a hex wrench, depending on the saw model. Push the notched shank of the blade as far as it will go up into the hollow portion of the reciprocating rod, then retighten the setscrew to anchor the blade.

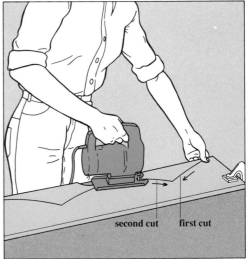

Cutting a curved pattern. Plan cuts so you will not force the blade through impossibly tight turns; here, both cuts move toward a sharp corner. Rest the tip of the shoe plate on the wood. Start the saw, and guide the blade into the wood, swinging the back of the saw right or left as you move into curves. Do not force the blade, lest it bind or break. If you end a cut with the blade in the wood, let it stop before withdrawing it.

The Circular Saw

The easiest way to get wood cut to size is to have it sawed at a lumberyard. To avoid this extra expense, however, you may decide to cut the pieces yourself, using a circular saw *(right)*. An inexpensive, compact and portable circular saw, though designed for rough carpentry, will cut the pieces for many projects with reasonable accuracy.

The standard circular saw for home use has a 7¼-inch blade that will cut through lumber up to 2 inches thick; for bevels, it tilts to any angle from 45° to 90°. To saw without binding, the motor should develop at least 1½ horsepower.

A variety of blades *(right)* is available for different cutting tasks. Carbide-tipped blades, although more expensive, will outlast ordinary steel blades and save money in the long run.

In operating the saw, a firm grip is extremely important. A 7¼-inch model weighs about 10 pounds and seems heavier when used at arm's length. For the added safety of a two-handed grip, buy a saw that has two handles.

A circular saw can be guided freehand for short cuts; for longer cuts, clamp a guide to the workpiece for accuracy *(right)*. The manufactured edge of ¼-inch plywood makes a good, straight guide. Always support lumber from below; without support, the board or panel may crack. Work the saw so that its heavy motor passes over the guide if you are using one.

Many accessories for circular saws are available at hardware stores. A patented metal guide can replace the wood straightedge shown at right. Another guide simplifies rip cutting. A circular-saw table, which holds a circular saw underneath it upside down, offers a few advantages of the professional's tool — stability and accuracy — at a lower price, but with some loss of versatility.

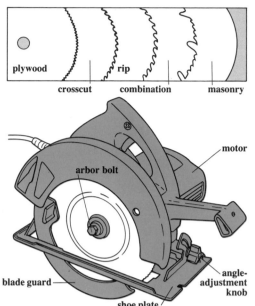

plywood   rip
crosscut   combination   masonry

motor
arbor bolt
blade guard
shoe plate
angle-adjustment knob

A circular saw. Driven by a powerful motor, the blade of a circular saw cuts on the upstroke. A spring-activated guard, which slides up into the housing of the saw during operation, drops back down over the blade as the cut is finished. The angle-adjustment knob lets the shoe plate be tilted for beveled cuts. The arbor bolt, which holds the blade in place, unscrews so that the blade can be changed.

Blade styles. A fine-toothed plywood blade slices through plywood without splintering it. A crosscut blade's small teeth tear smoothly across the grain; a ripping blade's larger teeth, set at a sharper angle, saw with the grain. A combination blade both rips and crosscuts, with small teeth separated by deep indentations. A toothless masonry blade scores brick and stone with its edge of abrasive silicon-carbide grit.

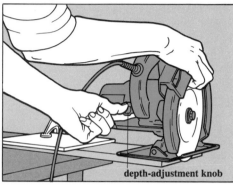

depth-adjustment knob

Adjusting blade depth. Loosen the depth-adjustment knob *(above)*. Lay the shoe plate flat on the wood and push up the blade guard. With one hand, hold up the guard while grasping the blade housing to support the saw body. Keeping the shoe plate flat, raise or lower the saw body — and with it the blade — until the blade is about ¼ inch below the bottom surface of the board to be cut. Retighten the depth-adjustment knob.

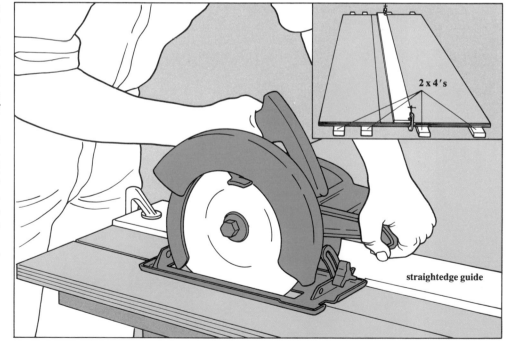

2 x 4's
straightedge guide

Sawing with a straightedge. Clamp a straightedge to the board to be cut so the blade falls on the waste side of the cutting line. Put on goggles before sawing. To cut a large panel of plywood *(inset)*, rest it on the floor, on 2-by-4s. Holding the saw firmly, cut slowly along the straightedge. Do not force the blade — it may bind. Keep a steady grip on the saw as it clears the board, and prepare to catch its unsupported weight.

The Variable-Speed Drill

Like the saber saw, the variable-speed drill works at a variety of speeds, depending on how hard you squeeze its trigger. Small holes in wood are bored at the fastest speeds; slower speeds are better for drilling large holes in wood and for any hole in metal or masonry.

The ⅜-inch drill at right can accommodate bit shanks from ¼₄ inch to ⅜ inch in diameter. Within that range, many different bits are available to drill holes from ¼₄ inch to 1½ inches in diameter in wood, metal or masonry. Power drills can also hold the shanks of such accessories as buffing wheels, grinding wheels and hole saws.

In this volume, the drill is most often used to drill the hole for a wood screw that fastens together two boards. This task actually requires three holes: one in the bottom board to grip the screw's threads tightly, and two successively wider holes in the top board for the shank and head. You can use a separate twist bit for each hole, then broaden the top hole with a countersink bit. More simply, you can bore all three holes at once with a counterbore bit, which matches the shape of the screw's threads and shank, and has an adjustable head that bores, or counterbores, a

recess for the screwhead. Avoid cheap counterbore bits: They tend to clog.

Spade bits bore holes up to 1½ inches in diameter; because these bits tend to wobble, use of a drill guide is advisable. The model at right, below, will fit any drill with a threaded shaft.

Masonry bits, with closely spaced, carbide-tipped edges, grind slowly through brick and concrete, which would crumble around a twist bit.

Masonry and spade bits are most often sold singly; countersinks are sold in only one size. Counterbore and twist bits are sold singly and in sets that include the most frequently used sizes.

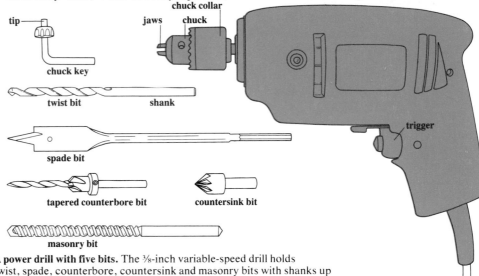

A power drill with five bits. The ⅜-inch variable-speed drill holds twist, spade, counterbore, countersink and masonry bits with shanks up to ⅜ inch in diameter. To insert a bit, turn the chuck collar to open the jaws, push the bit shank between the jaws and tighten the collar by hand until the jaws grip the shank. Then push the tip of the chuck key into one of the three holes in the chuck, and twist the key handle. To change bits, loosen the collar with the chuck key before turning it by hand.

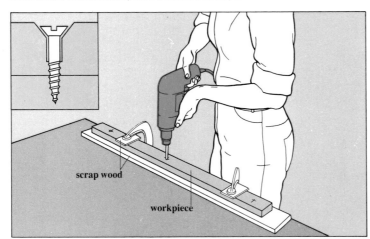

Using a power drill. Clamp the work to a table and indent the wood at the starting point with an awl. To govern a hole's depth, wrap tape around the bit at the required distance from the tip. Set the bit in the dent, squeeze the trigger and push the drill straight down with steady, moderate pressure. To drill holes for a wood screw *(inset)*, use a tapered counterbore bit *(above)*. Or drill two holes of increasing size, a narrow one in the bottom piece for the screw's threads and a wide one in the top for the shank. Widen the hole's mouth with a countersink bit if it will be puttied, or use a third twist bit if it will be plugged with a short dowel.

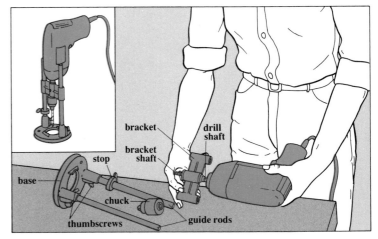

Attaching a drill guide. Remove the drill's chuck. (Most unscrew from the shaft of the drill, but check the manufacturer's instructions.) Twist the guide bracket onto the drill shaft; screw the chuck onto the bracket's shaft. Slip the guide rods through their holes in the bracket, loosen the thumbscrews on the base, set the ends of the rods flush with the bottom of the base, and tighten the screws; this procedure ensures that the holes drilled are perpendicular to the work surface when the drill guide is upright *(inset)*. If you want to drill to a certain depth, position the stop on the guide rod after you have inserted a bit in the chuck.

The Sewing Machine

One of the most ingenious home tools, the sewing machine is also one of the easiest to use and maintain. A good machine is virtually trouble-free mechanically and needs only a light oiling every three or four operating hours.

Threading the machine properly is essential; the owner's manual will tell you how. Although every model threads somewhat differently, there are always two threads, an upper thread from the spool and a lower thread wound around the bobbin *(right)*. The tension on the upper thread is adjusted with a knob.

Synthetic thread must be used with synthetic fabric, and natural with natural, so that, in cleaning, the fabric and thread shrink at the same rate. Size 50 thread and a size 14 needle are best for most fabrics, though heavier thread and a size 16 needle make stronger seams in thick fabric, such as canvas.

The number of stitches per inch also affects seam strength. The standard number is 12 to 15 stitches per inch, more if very strong seams are needed.

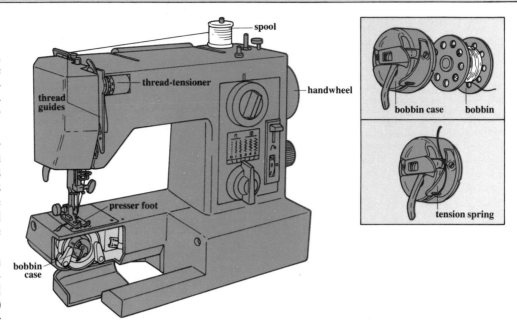

The versatile sewing machine. Every sewing machine has a set of thread guides that take the thread from the spool, through an adjustable thread-tensioner and down to the needle. A second thread is wound around a lower spool called the bobbin *(top inset)* and slipped underneath a tension spring *(bottom inset)* on the bobbin case.

Dials on the machine set the type, length and direction of a stitch. The presser foot, a ski-shaped clamp that holds the fabric flat, comes in a variety of configurations for special stitches. The feed dog, a toothed plate below the presser foot, advances the fabric automatically. The handwheel turns the mechanism to start the first stitch.

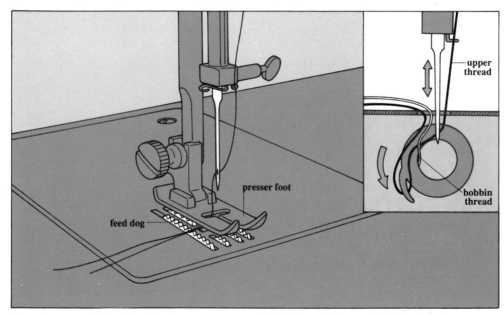

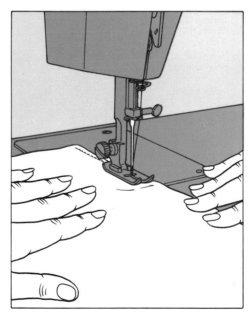

Preparing to sew. After threading the machine, lower the presser foot, grasp the end of the upper thread and turn the handwheel to make the first stitch. As you do this, the upper thread will tighten around the bobbin thread *(inset)* and pull it up in a loop. Raise the presser foot and pull out the end of the bobbin thread from the loop. Draw out both threads 3 or 4 inches and pull the ends together to the rear of the presser foot.

Sewing the fabric. Position the fabric under the needle. Lower the presser foot, turn on the machine, and guide the fabric as the feed dog pulls it forward. When you finish sewing, set the machine in reverse and backstitch over the last few stitches for reinforcement. Then raise the presser foot, pull out the fabric and cut both threads.

Acknowledgments

The index for this book was prepared by Louise Hedberg. The editors also wish to thank the following persons and institutions for their help in the preparation of this volume: Aquatic Garden Center, Jobston, New Jersey; Richard D. Baker, The King's Masons, Fairfax, Virginia; Aldo and Marirosa Ballo, Studio Ballo, Milan; James Birks, Silver Spring, Maryland; Heather Willson Cass, Cass & Pinnell Architects, Washington, D.C.; William Creager, Washington, D.C.; Lotte Dolezalek, Alexandria, Virginia; Keith Folsom, Lilypons Water Gardens, Lilypons, Maryland; Michael Glassman, Greenscapes and Graphics, Davis, California; Jolande and Lawrence Goldberg, Alexandria, Virginia; Rick Hansen, Baltimore Canvas Products Inc., Baltimore, Maryland; Leo Judej Jr., Annandale, Virginia; William J. Locklin, Loran, Inc., Redlands, California; Michael McKinley, Bolinas, California; Carl Mullins, Sundecks, Inc., Fairfax, Virginia; Wingate Paine, New York; Quality Fabricators, Bristow, Virginia; Frederick W. Sachs Jr., W. A. Smoot & Co., Inc., Alexandria, Virginia; Kirk Young Saunders, Outer Banks Deck Builders, Alexandria, Virginia; Charles Thomas, Lilypons Water Gardens, Lilypons, Maryland; James van Sweden, Oehme, van Sweden and Associates, Inc., Washington, D.C.; Mr. and Mrs. John M. Walton III, Spring House, Pennsylvania; Michael Wheeler, Alexandria, Virginia; Wicker World, McLean, Virginia.

Picture Credits

The sources for the photographs in this book are listed below, followed by the sources for the illustrations. Credits from left to right on a single page or a two page spread are separated by semicolons; credits from top to bottom are separated by dashes.

Photographs: **Cover:** Larry Sherer, photographer / table and chairs by Kartell, courtesy Placewares, Alexandria, Virginia / tableware, courtesy Portside, Alexandria, Virginia. **2, 3:** © Norman McGrath, photographer / Richard Dattner, architect, New York. **4:** Henry Groskinsky, photographer / Oehme, van Sweden & Associates, Inc., landscape architects, Washington, D.C. **5:** John Burwell, photographer / Lotte Dolezalek, designer, Alexandria, Virginia. **6:** © Norman McGrath, photographer / Peter Wilson, architect — Emmett Bright, photographer, Rome. **7:** Larry Sherer, photographer / William Creager, designer, Washington, D.C. **8, 9:** Carla De Benedetti, photographer, Milan / Luciano Grassi and Gastone del Greco, architects; Henry Groskinsky, photographer / Wingate Paine, designer, New York / John Mayer, landscape architect, New York. **10, 11:** Lisl Dennis, photographer / Betty Stewart, architectural designer, Santa Fe, New Mexico / Carolyn Fleig, stylist / furniture and china, courtesy Foreign Traders, Santa Fe, New Mexico / tableware, courtesy Table Talk, Santa Fe, New Mexico / basket, courtesy Canyon Road Flowers, Santa Fe, New Mexico. **22, 23:** Michael McKinley, photographer / hammock, courtesy Pawleys Island Hammocks, Pawleys Island, South Carolina / Thomas Baak and Associates, landscape architects, Walnut Creek, California / Chris Casale of Casale Homes, contractor, Blackhawk, California. **24:** Dan Cunningham, photographer / pillows, courtesy Rocky Road to Kansas, Alexandria, Virginia; Michael McKinley, photographer / hooks, courtesy Granny's Attic, Alexandria, Virginia / Thomas Baak and Associates, landscape architects, Walnut Creek, California / Chris Casale of Casale Homes, contractor, Blackhawk, California. **25:** Michael McKinley, photographer / ladder, courtesy Pawleys Island Hammocks, Pawleys Island, South Carolina / Thomas Baak and Associates, landscape architects, Walnut Creek, California / Chris Casale of Casale Homes, contractor, Blackhawk, California. **26.** Dan Cunningham, photographer / Oehme, van Sweden & Associates, Inc., landscape architects, Washington, D.C. **30, 34:** Dan Cunningham, photographer. **38:** Larry Sherer, photographer. **47-50:** Michael McKinley, photographer / lighting fixtures, courtesy Loran, Inc., Redlands, California / Jim Hagopian, landscape designer, Walnut Creek, California. **52:** Dan Cunningham, photographer / Richard D. Baker, mason, Fairfax, Virginia / furniture, courtesy Conran's, Washington, D.C. **60:** Dan Cunningham, photographer. **61:** Larry Sherer, photographer / Oehme, van Sweden & Associates, Inc., landscape architects, Washington, D.C. / James Birks, mason, Silver Spring, Maryland. **62:** Larry Sherer, photographer / pool, courtesy Coleco, Inc. **76, 77:** Larry Sherer, photographer / fountains, courtesy Lilypons Water Gardens, Lilypons, Maryland. **80:** John Burwell, photographer / Lotte Dolezalek, Lawrence and Jolande Goldberg, designers, Alexandria, Virginia. **88:** Dan Cunningham, photographer / John Walton III, designer, Spring House, Pennsylvania. **92:** Larry Sherer, photographer / Oehme, van Sweden & Associates, Inc., landscape architects, Washington, D.C. **93:** Jan Corash, photographer / Heather Willson Cass of Cass and Pinnell Architects, designer, Washington, D.C. **94:** Larry Sherer, photographer. **95:** Dan Cunningham, photographer. **96:** Larry Sherer, photographer / location, courtesy Dan Mason and John Russell, Alexandria, Virginia. **102:** Linda Bartlett, photographer / screen, courtesy Sundecks, Inc., Fairfax, Virginia. **109, 112:** Dan Cunningham, photographer. **116:** Dan Cunningham, photographer / wicker furniture, courtesy Wicker World, McLean, Virginia. *Illustrations:* **17:** Landscape design by Jane Krumbhaar, inked by John Massey. **18-21:** Landscape design by Jane Krumbhaar, artwork by Greg Harlin of Stansbury, Ronsaville, Wood, Inc. **23-25:** Sketches by Fred Holz, inked by John Massey. **27-29:** Sketches by Jack Arthur, inked by John Massey. **31-33:** Sketches by Roger Essley, inked by Elsie J. Hennig. **35-37:** Sketches by Fred Holz, inked by Eduino J. Pereira. **39-45:** Sketches by George Bell, inked by Stephen A. Turner. **46-50:** Sketches by William J. Hennessy Jr., inked by Frederic F. Bigio from B-C Graphics. **51:** Sketch by Fred Holz, inked by John Massey. **53-60:** Sketches by William J. Hennessy Jr., inked by Frederic F. Bigio from B-C Graphics. **61:** Sketch by Fred Holz, inked by Frederic F. Bigio from B-C Graphics. **63-73:** Sketches by George Bell, inked by Walter Hilmers Jr. from HJ Commercial Art. **74, 75:** Sketches by William J. Hennessy Jr., inked by John Massey. **76-79:** Sketches by David Baker, inked by Marc Levenson. **81-87:** Sketches by George Bell, inked by Stephen A. Turner. **89-95:** Sketches by Roger Essley, inked by Elsie J. Hennig. **97-101:** Sketches by George Bell, inked by Frederic F. Bigio from B-C Graphics. **103-108:** Sketches by Greg DeSantis, inked by John Massey. **109-111:** Sketches by William J. Hennessy Jr., inked by John Massey. **113-115:** Sketches by Jack Arthur, inked by John Massey. **117-121:** Sketches by Fred Holz, inked by Frederic F. Bigio from B-C Graphics. **122-125:** Sketches by Roger Essley, inked by Frederic F. Bigio from B-C Graphics.

Index

Time-Life Books Inc. offers a wide range of fine recordings, including a *Big Bands* series. For subscription information, call 1-800-621-7026, or write TIME-LIFE MUSIC, Time & Life Building, Chicago, Illinois, 60611.